Praise for

# Culture Leads Leaders Follow

"It takes courage to question the prevailing ethos of the day. In *Culture Leads Leaders Follow*, Al Sikes shares uncommon insight, wisdom and courage. I ended the book wishing he would run for national public office!"

> —Anne Adler, Former Executive Director,
> Young Women's Leadership Network, NYC

"In *Culture Leads Leaders Follow*, Al Sikes chronicles five decades of history, politic and communication technologies from a first person, up close and personal vantage point. Al Sikes definitely has been to the edge, and while there, gathered critical information for all of us. For all of those culture changers out there, those of you in the trenches, pushing very large rocks up very steep hills, read this book! Your time is coming!"

> —Gina Otto, Author of Cassandra's Angel and
> Founder & CEO Of Change My World Now

"When Al Sikes speaks, I have time to listen. Sikes shares his keen insights about the cultural influences and leadership demands around each of his diverse career experiences from small-town, mid-America through the challenging power struggles in Washington and on to the exhilarating scene in New York as a key player in the technological and financial transformation of our communications world."

> —Al McDonald, Former Global Managing Director,
> McKinsey and Company

*Culture Leads Leaders Follow*
by Al Sikes

Published by

◤ köehlerbooks™

210 60th Street
Virginia Beach, VA 23451
212-574-7939
www.koehlerbooks.com

*To Jenny and Brad,*
*Thank you for*
*pushing back.*

# Culture Leads
# Leaders Follow

## Al Sikes

VIRGINIA BEACH
CAPE CHARLES

# DEDICATION

This book is dedicated to my mother, Marcia Weber Sikes and my father, William Kendall Sikes who taught me the boundaries of self.

And especially to my wife, Marty, whose presence is a continual reminder of the importance of love.

# TABLE OF CONTENTS

# FOREWORD

WHEN I FIRST MET Al Sikes, I knew him as the emcee at the Monty Alexander Jazz Festival in Easton, Maryland. I knew him as the man dressed in a simple blue suit and as the name on the box seats. It wasn't until weeks later that someone clued me in that Al was not only the festival founder, but also chairman of the Federal Communications Commission (FCC) during the Bush Administration and a nationally recognized social entrepreneur.

The next time we met, I felt uneasy in conversation, eking out words ever so carefully. He perceived the situation otherwise and effortlessly uncovered our shared interests: jazz, art, China, communication.

This mild-mannered man sitting across from me—speaking slowly, clearly, deliberately—said little of himself unless prompted, but when he did, his stories were profoundly straightforward. When I asked him how he pursued his wife, Marty, he told me that it was pretty simple, really. He met her. He liked her. He asked her out for ice cream. The rest was history. It was like the way he slipped into the role of beekeeping-tractor-driver while the two of us toured around his farm's private wetlands one crisp fall day. Or when he told me how, at a young age, he had found an honest, humble, fearless mentor who later opened for him a career door.

My professional life is not a political one; professionally speaking, Al and I have very little overlap. Except for our work's mutual emphasis on culture. In Al's work with media—particularly via the FCC and The Hearst Corporation—and my work in the arts, we recognize the significance both sectors have in societal development and human flourishing. Music makes us move. Images connect the dots. Words make concrete that which we long to know as reality. Dance is a celebration of life. Beauty helps us breathe. And while politics and the elite influence laws which govern our culture, it's the culture itself that ultimately shapes society.

In this memoir, *Culture Leads, Leaders Follow,* Al Sikes narrates his time in a seat of cultural influence. Unexpected, even counterintuitive opportunities to those he had conceived for himself "invited [him] to join and at times lead a revolution." Moving from small-town Missouri to arguably America's most powerful cities—Washington D.C. and New York City—where aggression is the expectation and *no* is not an option, Al learned to become a coherent voice of morality, one that would question the way our culture operates and how it might be radically changed. Take, for example, his altercation with Howard Stern in the 1989 push against "indecent broadcasting" and Stern's abuse of free speech.

Even when recounting morally besmirched situations, the stories in these pages, not unlike his blue emcee's suit, are clean, well pressed and confidently donned. They are moments in history articulated comfortably by the writer, a man reserved in the details, saturated in character, and sharp in opinion. A man of entrepreneurial spirit, Al writes not as a way to record his life, to reflect on his career, or to out the juicy specifics of his political past. He writes to envision a world for the future generations of leaders, to present possibilities for the storytellers to come.

*Culture Leads, Leaders Follow* is an edgy and pointed assessment that critically addresses free markets, media, technology, faith in the public square, and fatherhood. Though written by a leader whose celebrity began almost 25 years ago, it's not a book for the power brokers of the 1990s and the early 2000s. Rather, it's one for today's young leaders who are attempting to creatively navigate the legacy of a convoluted culture left by previous generations, despite the temptation to submit to its unchallenged flow. It is a picture of what it looks like to be the leader we should want to be, even when we feel underqualified or too small for the position ahead. It points us to an honest, humble, fearless kind of success. The kind of success that can imagine new and outrageous things for a clamorous culture fighting for resolve.

—Chelsea A. Horvath

# INTRODUCTION

SOME YEARS AGO A friend greeted me saying, "You used to be Al Sikes, didn't you?" Lloyd Meeds, who served a number of terms in Congress from Washington State, captured the moment with deft humor. I had a year or so earlier ended my tenure as Chairman of the Federal Communications Commission (FCC). In Washington's hierarchy I had gone from somebody to nobody. Sure, people still took my calls, but many of my "friends" had moved on to the next office holder.

I had also moved on. Lloyd's irreverent question arrived at the end of my first year living and working in Manhattan. I now understand that my Washington and New York gigs equipped me with new lenses. It is as if an optometrist layered prescriptive lenses to help me see more clearly.

I arrived in Washington in 1986 with Midwestern sensibilities. I left Washington with a much tougher hide and a more skeptical attitude. New York added layers of both and a characteristic question: What is the bottom line?

In quite different ways my job at the FCC and the media work I did in New York put me in the middle of culture making. Along the way I found that most creative people and their bosses seem to have little interest in the broader consequences of their radio show or record or TV sitcom or whatever expressions, or how they help shape popular culture. Unfortunately, today's popular culture often pulls against our best instincts.

If you want to perplex dinner guests, ask them how they would define culture and who they think influences it and how. Then, in the context of today's presidential campaign, ask what cultural phenomena gave rise to the popularity of Donald Trump, Ben Carson and Bernie Sanders. Each candidate, as I write, has enjoyed the support of at least a quarter to a third of their respective party's faithful–added up that is a lot of people.

I began *Culture Leads Leaders Follow* many years before the 2016 presidential race and many years after my friend noted I used to be Al Sikes. In the meantime I have left the workaday world, begun beekeeping with my wife Marty and started a jazz festival in my home town of Easton, Maryland.

But, I am no less intrigued by cultural formation, how it influences us and how it shapes those who purport to be leaders. And, since faith is an important part of my life, that lens is added as I strive to find some clarity in both my life and the human condition.

*Culture Leads Leaders Follow* traces my work and at times confrontations with Washington's establishment and those who seek its favors. My education continued in Manhattan where the hinge of my job was disruptive media.

It became evident from the very outset that my life in Washington and then New York would exist in a swirl of aggression–more aggression than I anticipated. As the disruptive potential of new technologies became more evident, the force field of the swirl felt like one of those Midwestern tornadoes I had left behind.

I highlight episodes with such characters as Howard Stern, Rupert Murdoch, Al Gore, President Jimmy Carter, Supreme Court Justice Clarence Thomas, Mark Cuban and Jack Valenti while comparing and contrasting them with the guiding influences in my own life. Fortunately for me, those influences include a number of gifted young leaders whose work in their communities and beyond are cause for hope.

Perhaps, just perhaps, *Culture Leads Leaders Follow* will start some conversations and spur some initiatives that will be influential in shaping a more beneficent culture. I even provide some questions at the end of the book which I believe you will find provocative. So, enjoy the book and if you want to include me in the conversation, bring your voice to alsikes.com.

# TIME ZONES AND LEADERSHIP

*Men are qualified for civil liberty in exact proportion*
*to their disposition to put moral chains upon their own*
*appetites... Society cannot exist unless a controlling*
*power upon will and appetite be placed somewhere,*
*and the less of it there is within, the more there must*
*be without. It is ordained in the eternal constitution of*
*things that men of intemperate minds cannot be free.*
*Their passions forge their fetters.*

**Irish-born philosopher Edmund Burke**

I remember the winter of 1985 as especially harsh, the kind of chill that you don't forget. Washington's damp and penetrating cold is like that.

I had flown to Washington on a gray December day from St. Louis to meet with the Secretary of Commerce in President Reagan's Administration, Malcolm Baldrige. His office was warm—the Secretary had an employee that kept the fireplace well stoked.

I was meeting with Secretary Baldrige about a job. The White House had told Baldrige that President Reagan was prepared to nominate me to head the National Telecommunications and Information Administration, a job in the Commerce Department, if he approved.

Baldrige, whose nickname was Mac, was in his mid-60s, tall, lean and thoroughly plainspoken. His sister, Letitia, who had been Jacqueline Kennedy's social secretary, wrote books on etiquette. Mac didn't read them.

Mac, whose body was somewhat bent, was often more cowboy than Cabinet secretary. His hobby was calf-roping and he was still entering rodeos at age sixty-four.

It was said that Mac would only take a call on the first try from the president and "any cowboy." This folklore about the man behind the big desk turned out to be instructive.

I had entered Mac's office with at least a slight trepidation. Prospects were quickly giving way to realities and, for me, selling a broadcast business I had started in 1978 and moving to Washington would be a wrenching change. My first 45 years had been in small towns and cities in Missouri where, by contrast, ambitions were more modest, power-based cleavages fewer and accomplishments often understated.

• • •

I grew up being told, and then believing, that America was exceptional. It had helped transform Harry S. Truman from a machine politician in Kansas City, Missouri, into an international leader. Then, Dwight David Eisenhower came home after leading the Allied Forces in World War II to serve two terms as President. His leadership talents and caliber were not in doubt.

My formative years were enriched by stories of Truman, a home state president, and Eisenhower. They, responding to a deeper set of values, led America in peacekeeping while providing international assistance to the people ravaged by war.

And my parents made sure I attended Sunday School, where sin and the possibility of redemption were featured.

At the earliest cognitive moment in my life, I became familiar with my Dad's necessary service—fighting Fascism on foreign shores. Dad had joined virtually all males of his generation and fought in the Asian Theater in World War II. He served as an enlisted man.

Dad's generation then built an extraordinary engine of prosperity. The economic engine mostly produced goods and services that improved lives. Most people had to work hard to satisfy needs and consumer credit was not yet flowing. Mom and Dad saved and saved and saved, and finally built a house. True discretionary spending was a modest part of the economy; savings were more notable.

By the time I started down my professional path, I was certainly academically and religiously familiar with human weakness. As a student at Westminster College in Fulton, Missouri, I had studied political science, history and philosophy. As a law student at the University of Missouri, I had looked at several centuries of case studies detailing man's inhumanity and the court's reaction.

But by the time I finished law school in 1964, America was at a new beginning. It was on a trajectory that in many ways was far different both culturally and economically from my first two decades.

As I look back now, the early narratives in my life were about character. World War II and America's leadership in helping to rebuild war-torn countries provided dramatic lessons of character. The end of all my father and mother's stories and admonitions was about character. And the narratives of the popular culture in the 1950s and 60s were mostly not at war with the upstream influences in my life—the influences that flowed from family, teachers and the church. There were cultural tensions—rock and roll supplied the primary irritant—but the cleavages were much less pronounced.

• • •

I was no longer young—or impressionable—when I arrived at Secretary Baldrige's office. An abrupt change in my attitudes or approaches was not going to happen.

Baldrige occupied a gymnasium-sized office that featured old-school elegance and was decidedly male in adornments. It was, I must admit, at least somewhat intimidating.

The Secretary was seated behind his desk. Beside his desk was a very large horse saddle. Mac wanted his visitors to know that they were across the table from one tough dude. I have been in a lot of A-list offices, but this was the most distinctive, and its occupant the most unique. Ronald Reagan was often portrayed as a horseback rider—presumably to show he was earthy and rugged. And I know a lot of people who ride horses. But Mac Baldrige is the only one I have known that while riding a horse at a rapid speed lassoed a large running calf, dismounted and then rushed forward to tie off three legs.

Mac was from Connecticut—not rodeo country. His pedigree was in manufacturing—not politics. As I got to know him, it was clear that he had little patience with Washington's hyper-political jockeying. He was a pragmatist and more doctrinaire arguments made him angry.

On that decidedly cold December morning, Secretary Baldrige stayed behind his desk as I entered his office. After the barest of greetings, he said, "Washington is a god-damned tough town. Everybody is after a piece of your ass. How do you rate yourself for aggressiveness?"

The question ended, silence followed, and I then put the best face I could on my own aggressiveness. I had managed political campaigns and built a business using significant levels of debt, I explained, and then went on to note that there were lines I would not cross. There was no discussion of which lines. I think we both knew what the unspoken meant.

Welcome to Washington. Or it could have been welcome to New York City, my next stop, seven years later. I had started that morning in Springfield, Missouri, my home, but it was as if I had crossed more than one time zone. And as I would increasingly learn on a personal level, the power cities are awash in aggression—"survival of the fittest" is the creed.

• • •

As I reflect on my relationship with Mac, I can vividly recall a conversation on the way to the White House. Looking out the window of his chauffeured town car on a hot and humid August day in Washington, I quipped that we were fortunate not to be tourists walking from site to site. He shot back, "I would rather be doing that than going to the White House for one more debate over my recommendations to the president." Domestic policy options had to be vetted by The Economic Policy Council (EPC) before they could be sent to the president. The EPC, headed by then-Secretary of the Treasury James Baker, was not a venue for the faint of heart or, for that matter, the pragmatic.

• • •

By the time Mac had stripped away the veneer of Washington pleasantries, I was in default mode. *No* was not an option. My close friend, mentor and occasional employer, Senator John C. Danforth, (R-Missouri), had opened a door. I couldn't go soft. I had to at least masquerade as a power-city capable leader.

My meeting with Mac and subsequent work with him occurred over a generation ago. President Reagan, then President George H. W. Bush, and still later Frank A. Bennack Jr., the CEO of The Hearst Corporation in New York, afforded me a rare opportunity. I was invited to join—and at times lead—a revolution in communications and information technologies while getting an intimate view of life at the top of America's power cities.

We entered the 21st century enthralled with the promises of technology. Now we are awash in devices, channels and software services and the challenges, not just the benefits, they present.

More recently, President Obama spoke eloquently about a more elevated approach to politics. Yet political cleavages have rarely been deeper or sharper.

While my voice draws on experiences dating back to the 1950s, it has been more shaped by the last two decades. And it is not written for people who held power in the 1990s or even in the first decade of the 21st Century. It is the long game that concerns me.

• • •

In recent years my life's perspective has been broadened and sharpened by a number of younger friends. I have had the good fortune to work with exceptional young leaders on a range of for-profit and not-for-profit enterprises. I hope this book turns out to be insightful to those much younger than my peers.

But I cannot go forward without a disclaimer. In moments of reflection I am often reminded of the poet Robert Burns, who warned:

*And would some Power the small gift give us*
*To see ourselves as others see us!*
*It would from many a blunder free us,*
*And foolish notion:*
*What airs in dress and gait would leave us,*
*And even devotion!*

I sought power, held it and used it. Undoubtedly, I did not always use it with the full considerations that we should expect of those who hold public office. Inevitably, as Burns notes, humans have an impossible time being fully objective about themselves.

# THE ISSUE

*...in civil society as well as in government we are in an age of empty suits and stylish haircuts on hollow heads.*

**Walter Russell Mead, Bard College professor**

*The only real revolution is in the enlightenment of the mind and the improvement of character, the only real emancipation is individual and the only real revolutionists are philosophers and saints.*

**Will Durant, American writer and philosopher**

Trout have a lot to teach humanity.

Trout thrive where the water is clean, clear and cold. Where we pollute the water, trout disappear.

One of my joys is to cast a wisp of a fly into the current of a mountain stream where trout stalk insects that float on the water. Fly fishing is sport in paradise. If I proceed quietly, make an accurate cast and allow no tension on the floating line, my prospect for a thrilling strike increases dramatically.

A not so subtle prerequisite of success in landing a wild and wary trout is the quality of the leader. The leader is the last length of line—the lead line—and is slight and transparent in appearance, but does not break easily.

If the leaders are too short or thick, the trout will sense deception and not rise to the fly. If the leader is frayed, I might well hook the trout but lose it in the ensuing fight. In this world of competitive engagement between fish and man, the leader is crucial. The trout provides immediate and unambiguous feedback.

*Leader* is a complex word. It defines the tip of a fishing line and also a person who has followers. I have had experience with both. Rarely is the human version as slight and transparent in appearance as the fishing line. Television favors the opposite, often the preening or bombastic and obvious.

Followership for all of us begins early. Our parents lead us. Teachers lead us, or at least try to, and on and on.

But then later, we look at our lives and wonder what happened. Most lives are not predictable—they do not follow a linear path. And not infrequently, we are disappointed with how things turn out. In our more reflective moments, we even search for cause and effect.

Now, at the risk of giving trout more prominence than they deserve, let me return to the stream and look up river as a trout does. Their food, often small insects, rides the currents as it moves downstream.

The trout is instinctive. It surveys a few square feet for its food while remaining acutely aware of shadows. Osprey and mergansers, among other fish-eating birds, are an overhead threat. Otters and other fish-eating mammals come from the side or below.

If a trout was all appetite, it would quickly become prey. The same can be said of humans.

It didn't take long for me to find myself in the world of outsized appetites after moving from a small city in Missouri to Washington and then to New York City to join the media industry.

The power cities featured many shades of gray and angles of light or dark. And these were far from the straightforward shadows of the stream world. In both mega-cities, the angles of light and dark were manipulated skillfully. It was an art form and often pursued by those with overweening ambitions.

Manipulation, of course, breeds suspicion. I must admit that, beyond the excitement of the moment, having to frequently look over my shoulder was not appealing. I constantly dealt with people who were driven to win every game, regardless of costs. That exacts a toll. As trust in relationships ebbed, I felt an erosion of my own humanity. Frequent skepticism and impatience are not endearing traits.

It also became clear that leadership was often just theater. Politicians pandered, while those that were in Washington to influence them made lavish use of flattery. When dealing with the vain, never discount the power of flattery.

Flattery assumed a different shape in Manhattan. If a business or show or application was both distinctive and popular, it was immediately copied. Profit—not originality—was the driving force.

In both cities the lowest common denominator was often the most powerful economic, political and ultimately, cultural force. Appetites were identified and serving them became key elements in election campaigns and business models—too often the only forces.

In New York, a variety of media were used in race-to-the-bottom narratives that fed voyeurism, while several hundred miles to the south, in Washington, most politicians were using the US Treasury as an extension of their campaign funds.

Much of today's prevailing disquiet traces not to real leaders, but to ones who specialize in pandering, whether in politics or business. And I would suggest that we, the followers, can see pandering leadership coming. A trout would not be fooled—it recognizes the shadows. Yet while most pandering has become an easily discerned shadow, we still have a hard time resisting.

I do not approach either cause or effect as an academic. I am a practitioner who spent much of the sweet spot of my career among the elite, swimming the big waters of Washington and New York. In Washington, I chaired the Federal Communications Commission and, in New York, I directed venture capital investments and new digital business start-ups for The Hearst Corporation, a large privately held media company.

It can, of course, be argued that only those who stand apart can honestly critique. But those who have not felt the forces— the driving pressures of ambition in a hothouse environment— too often are simply theorists. Those who have felt the forces have almost inevitably yielded to them at times. Winning is not a luxury—it is required. Indeed as incentives and motivations get scrambled, and when the culture offers very little resistance, rationalization becomes easier and easier.

Without question, personal ambition and leadership drive both results and progress. There are characteristics of bygone cultures—for which many are nostalgic. But I do not know anybody who would like to turn the clock back on racial equality, for example. Or medicine. Or a range of things that make life more just and pleasant.

Yet the disquiet that pervades society today is not fanciful. It is both cerebral and heart-felt. If the body politic in America could hire an executive search firm, it would reject both political parties and their leaders. We wouldn't have to wait for the next election.

Our political institutions, which exist to protect life, liberty and happiness, are about as popular as a colonoscopy. And this is at a moment in history when society's complexities and challenges are intense. Truth be told, much of the intensity results from decisions now understood to have been largely self-serving or skewed toward special interests.

But the dangers and challenges we face go well beyond the home front. If you hold your nation out as a compelling example to the world—and we do—then your institutions must function well and produce a high level of public satisfaction. Our failings are used skillfully by our competitors like China, our adversaries like Russia, and online jihadists who recruit people willing to die for their benighted beliefs. Humanity is the target.

*Humanity* is, of course, a big word—perhaps too big. The clashes around how it can best be served are deafening. Yet too many who work the levers of business power, perhaps most, turn away from any real attempt to measure their actions against a more elevated standard than simply profit. They yield to market economics or, for those seeking a government job, political calculus. If required, power brokers dress their actions up with phrases like "We are serving market demand" or "We are listening to the voters" (read: checking the polls)—this is ambition unhinged from more elevated values.

Often market demand serves only lowest common denominator appetites, whether commercial or political. Those appetites become a proxy for humanity. They are too small.

• • •

Few countries afford more opportunity for individual leadership than the United States. Much of the world is organized more hierarchally. Tyrants punish individual leadership and, through top-down economic systems, incentivize cronyism and target political opponents and business outliers. Russia, in the last twenty years, has provided a vivid example as she moved from Yeltsin's oligarchs to Putin's, and their government enablers and protectors.

Americans and the immigrants that join us enjoy an extraordinary legacy of farsighted leadership. Our primary civil institutions are at least legally and structurally strong, if not always operationally adept. However, there has been a big shift in both domestic and global economies. Today, disquiet is the prevailing mood and self-regard often the prevailing motivation.

Personal consumption has increasingly become the driving force of both the economy and the culture. As of December 2012, personal consumption was 71 percent of our annual gross domestic product (GDP) compared to a long-term average of 66 percent. Much of what we buy, of course, is imported. Our trade deficit, funded by debt, is huge. And while the growth in imports assures lower prices, it also destroys lower value-added jobs.

In many ways, we have become increasingly organized around growth in personal consumption. Government and business alike see growth as the end and take whatever steps their constantly shifting set of leaders think will achieve that end.

Material or electoral success tends to frame the lineup of leaders, almost regardless of their insight or the longer-term soundness of their plans. Yet persons who occupy those leadership categories—regardless of their talent—are most likely responding to cultural incentives. And the cultural incentives are increasingly consumerist ones.

At the ground level, it is often the purchase of things we don't need. Marketers specialize in spinning tales of material glory that can be ours if we will just buy the latest copy of whatever.

Celebrity wealth is glamorized. In this oxygen-rich atmosphere, enough is too often not enough. While conspicuous consumption has always been around, never has it been more conspicuous. In our noisy society, media amplifiers are plugged into the rich, the famous and, not infrequently, the scandalized.

And in politics, we confront an orgy of spending other people's money. Why re-prioritize public spending when more taxes on casino revenue or now taxes on marijuana sales will defer the cost question beyond the next election cycle?

Most leaders, it turns out, are aggressive followers and increasingly appetite-led. The heart or soul is largely unattended. Character, too often, yields to the lowest common denominator.

My life has given me a chance to observe national leadership up close and personal. And some of my more insightful friends and colleagues have helped me think more clearly about what leadership is and isn't.

Also, being intimately involved with the rapid evolution and disruption by technology has often refocused my mind on first principles. I arrived in a number-please world where telephone operators connected callers. Today, connections are handled robotically across an international network of fiber, radio frequencies, and devices. But along with these marvels, cyber-warfare has become an existential threat while the youthful infatuation with violent video games and social networks worries everybody who does not sell them.

Our stream of life is filled with shadows. Unfortunately, too often, we are prey.

# BEGINNINGS

*He sometimes felt that he had missed his life*
*By being far too busy looking for it.*
*Searching the distance, he often turned to find*
*That he had passed some milestone unaware,*
*And someone else was walking next to him,*
*First friends, then lovers, now children and a wife.*

*He noticed then that no one chose the way—*
*All seemed to drift by some collective will.*
*The path grew easier with each passing day,*
*Since it was worn and mostly sloped downhill.*
*The road ahead seemed hazy in the gloom.*
*Where was it he had meant to go, and with whom?*

**Dana Gioia, American poet and writer**

Almost always, part of our world-views can be traced back. Mine were rooted just north of the geographical boot in Southern Missouri.

In the summer of 1956, I was fifteen. My parents, Marcia and Kendall Sikes, lived in Southeast Missouri in a small town named Sikeston.

The name Sikeston originated with my colorful great-great-great-uncle, John Turner Sikes. He had declared a very modest piece of land and associated buildings Sikes' Town in 1860, just ahead of the Civil War.

He owned the general store, which included the saloon. Sometimes while watching a Western movie, I feel like I am being given glimpses of his store. As it turned out, selling general merchandise and liquor didn't work well. One day, a drunk had to be thrown out. As my uncle turned to re-enter the store, he was shot and killed. Unfortunately, Wyatt Earp was just a teenager then, too young and too far away to clean out the bad guys in Sikes Town.

Sikeston was just twenty-one miles north of New Madrid. New Madrid had been the Confederate capital of Missouri during the Civil War and the principal crop in Southeast Missouri was cotton.

Late that summer of 1956, and just days before school started, my dad taught me the most important lesson I learned as a teenager. He pulled me aside and we had one of those serious father-son conversations. Father talked—son listened.

"The talk around town," he began "is that a large group of parents and others will attempt to close down Sikeston High School on its opening day. At the very least, they will demonstrate against the integration of the student body and will try to get as many as possible to boycott... You will go to school."

I was starting my eleventh year in school and had not occupied a class with a black student. Brown v. Board of Education, which ruled segregation unconstitutional, was decided by the US Supreme Court in 1954. Sikeston was now voluntarily integrating, but on an incremental basis. A year later, just to our south, Arkansas Governor Orval Faubus used his state's National Guard to block the integration of Central High School in Little Rock. President Eisenhower sent in the 101st Airborne Division and nationalized the Arkansas National Guard to force integration.

Sikeston, economically and culturally, was more Arkansas than Missouri—more Southern than Midwestern. Many schools in the area still stopped school for "cotton picking vacations" during the fall harvest. Having walked on my knees picking cotton, I can tell you it was no vacation. And segregation was a first principle of the underlying culture.

The demonstration that opening day of school proved loud and raucous. Then the bus bringing the black students arrived—the insulting rant grew louder. As I recall, several hundred lined up on either side of the entrance walk that went up to the school steps. I remember having a certain pride as I walked, along with a dozen or so black students, through the chanters.

Dad had put his public and private life at risk. He gave me my first lesson in courage. Many of the demonstrators were customers of Sikes Hardware Store and had voted for him to be a member of the City Council.

Time has provided me a fuller measure of respect for what I suspect many will regard as a modest act. Dad was acting against his self-interest. He was rebelling against the culture where he lived and worked. He was doing the right thing. His action told me that leadership is not about getting re-elected or improving your sales, but about doing what is right.

My dad chose not to take the downhill slope and gave me an especially intimate look at real leadership, three months before my sixteenth birthday—his leadership, my north star.

North stars burn brightly and perpetually. My dad has been gone for almost twenty years, but I can still hear his words of caution or encouragement. Today's culture tends to produce a cascade of blazing meteors as our fleeting attention span searches for the new, new thing.

Lest I leave this formative moment in 1956 without acknowledging another one that occurred five years later, please allow me a word on my marriage.

I have enjoyed the blessings of a sublime marriage. My wife, Marty, also grew up in the Midwest. She spent her childhood in the headwaters of the Mississippi while I was about 500 miles downstream. Her homes were in Minnesota and Wisconsin.

Of course, the most telling gift of a sublime marriage is love. My wife has a PhD in love, which has both influenced me and softened my competitive nature.

# REVOLUTIONARY LEADERSHIP

*I am convinced that we will never build a democratic state based on rule of law if we do not at the same time build a state that is—regardless of how unscientific this may sound to the ears of a political scientist—humane, moral, intellectual, and spiritual, and cultural. The best laws and the best-conceived democratic mechanisms will not in themselves guarantee legality or freedom or human rights—anything, in short, for which they were intended—if they are not underpinned by certain human and social values.*

**Vaclav Havel, Czech writer, philosopher, and first President of the Czech Republic**

Politics did not, for me, begin that winter morning in 1985 in Secretary Baldrige's office. Few laboring outside of it are interviewed by the White House Personnel Office and later by a cabinet secretary.

The doors to the White House and Secretary of Commerce

offices had been opened for me by the Chairman of the Senate Commerce Committee, John C. Danforth. It is helpful to have a friend to whom the White House must pay attention. Washington jobs don't go to those who lack political support. I was not the inevitable right candidate for the job at the end of a painstaking executive search. Connections and associated power were much more important than my resume.

"Jack," as friends to the senator called him, and I were both political and real friends. Our friendship began in 1968.

I had gotten to know Jack during his improbable campaign for Attorney General. He ran against the Democrat incumbent, Norman Anderson, but more importantly, he challenged the political machine, which had controlled state politics in Missouri for 30 years and turned its government into a one-party fief.

The Republican Party was in desperate need of resuscitation. Jack, however, didn't need Party money—there was none. Jack's grandfather, William H. Danforth, founded the Ralston-Purina Company and his wealth allowed Jack to run an independent and well-financed campaign.

Odds aside, he won and the following day sent a cablegram to me in Argentina—where I was at a conference—asking me to become an assistant attorney general.

I had just been made a partner in a law firm, was comfortable and looked forward to being more comfortable. Jack was asking me to leave an increasingly good law practice in Springfield, Missouri and move to the state capital. I said no. A week later he phoned and I said no again, but did agree to fly to Missouri's capital, Jefferson City, the day after Thanksgiving to meet with a small group that was planning the transition. That Friday turned out to be one of the most pivotal days in my young life. I was 29.

Jack was very persuasive. He knew my weakness and got quickly to the point. After a few minutes of telling me about the transition plans, he said, "You don't understand my offer. I am not asking you to become just an assistant attorney general; I want you to join a handful of us to turn Missouri government around. We will elect the next Governor in 1972," he concluded. Revolution was in the air and my pulse certainly quickened.

I couldn't decline the reformulated invitation and began a deep dive into new possibilities and opportunities. Among other things, I was invited to learn about power and leaders' use of it on the inside—I ceased being a spectator.

On the day Jack was inaugurated, there were four of us who joined him in Jefferson City, Missouri's Capital, which sits on the banks of the Missouri River and is in between Missouri's biggest cities, St. Louis and Kansas City. While over time a dozen or so, including Clarence Thomas, the future Supreme Court Justice, eventually joined this counter-establishment cadre, it remained at its core a small group. Yet it succeeded in government and then in politics. Jack's movement elected Christopher "Kit" Bond Missouri Auditor in 1970 and then governor in 1972.

While I had flirted with running for office, I was just as comfortable being in the background. I ended up managing Jack Danforth's first campaign for the US Senate (he lost) and in 1976 Kit Bond's successful campaign for Governor.

By today's standards those campaigns were inexpensive. An industry has since emerged to recruit and sell candidates at extraordinary expense, funded mostly by interests with detailed wish lists. At the presidential level, seven-figure gifts to campaigns through political action committees (PACs) have become disturbingly familiar. This commercialization of government begs for a counter-revolution led by plainspoken leaders who align themselves with best governance practices and then follow them. But as government's size and intrusiveness grow, there is little prospect that one or another form of aggressive special interest leverage and advocacy will not keep pace and be constitutionally protected.

Jack hired on merit. The attorney general's legal opinions were issued without partisan favoritism. State agency representation was used to end or blunt corrupt practices, such as issuing bank and insurance company charters to political supporters.

Jack was one of the first attorneys general to use the law creatively to achieve results that had generally been achieved through elections. Politically favored banks had received millions in state deposits and were allowed, by patronage appointees, to keep the dollars in demand accounts that did not earn interest for the taxpayers. Jack sued the banks for Missouri taxpayers and asked for interest on a high percentage of deposits. He won.

We were called the *Holier than Thou* boys, drawing on our youth and Jack's other face as an Episcopalian priest. He had earned law and divinity degrees from Yale. As I look back, I am sure that our growing confidence and assertiveness did at times become arrogant.

The governor's office and the Missouri legislature tried to cripple the attorney general's office through reduced appropriations and attempts at narrowing our jurisdictional reach. Some of the obstacles were even amusing. I led several investigations against corrupt officials and asked for an unofficial license plate for our investigator's undercover work. The patronage-ridden Department of Revenue issued one with the number CIA-007.

Recollections are far from perfect, but my mind locates a seminal moment and lesson in real leadership in the first month of Danforth's term. One day the two of us were discussing a draft Attorney General's Opinion I had prepared regarding the constitutional parameters of the Lieutenant Governor's role as presiding officer over the Missouri Senate.

While we met, Jack received a call from an official with Ralston Purina, the company that sold feed for animals and cereal for people and is now owned by Nestle. As noted, Purina had been founded by Jack's grandfather, and the Danforth family had significant ownership interests. Also, Purina had expanded into the fast food business; it owned the Jack-in-the-Box hamburger franchise. The call, from a Purina official, confirmed the accuracy of a pending consumer complaint. The complaint stated that Jack-in-the-Box had soy meal in what it advertised as all-beef patties.

At Westminster College, where I had gone to undergraduate school, I had majored in political science, and if I learned nothing else, I learned that most politics is pulled along by self-interest. Most politicians follow the formula: reward your friends, punish your enemies and always look through the lens of the next election. In my few minutes of listening to Jack's side of the conversation, I heard the opposite. Jack's actions were my dad's writ large.

It would have been relatively easy for Jack to find a quiet face-saving angle for Purina. Instead he told his opposite number on the phone that he had a week to agree to a public admission of wrongdoing and pay a fine or a lawsuit would be filed. Today, because we have an inherent distrust in all things political, Jack would be required to recuse himself. But as I began to learn, in Attorney General Danforth's office, the unorthodox was frequently the orthodox.

Character co-existed with power and ambition. It was more than a paragraph in a speech or a line in a political commercial. Missourians had elected a strong leader and he would lead a reformation in Missouri government. I was very fortunate to hold my first government office as an employee of Jack Danforth.

When Jack called in 1968, I had resisted. But what I got when I finally said yes was an insider's view of revolutionary leadership. I cannot imagine a more enlightening experience. And what Jack predicted happened. Kit Bond, a fellow assistant attorney general, ran for governor in 1972 and was elected.

Kit's victory in November 1972 resulted in my directing the transition from Governor Warren Hearnes to Kit and then serving in the new governor's cabinet. My principal cabinet role was as Director of the Missouri Department of Consumer Affairs, Regulation and Licensing. I will spare you the details on how this combination of government agencies ended up in the same department, but a fair amount of my oversight involved bank and insurance regulation.

I also enjoyed my close association with Kit. From the Governor's office, Kit continued the reform work Jack began. And perhaps most notably, used his political capital to re-organize an often corrupt and inefficient government while his opponent was attacking him for a rise in utility energy prices caused by the Arab oil embargo. Many believe that Kit's tenacious focus on reform cost him the election in 1976. He was re-elected Governor in 1980 and then to the US Senate in 1986.

• • •

By 1976, I knew it was time to move on. Many of my friends and associates who had entered government with energy, ideals and enthusiasm were frequently talking about what government job they might next hold or seek. That was not a path I wanted to follow.

For four years, I had been telling businesses what they could or could not do. It was time for me to experience business on the other side. While I had a law degree and seven years in either private or public practice, I felt the pull of the Sikes family business genes.

The big question: okay there is a pull, but in what direction?

As a teenager I had flirted with the possibility of going to the University of Missouri and majoring in broadcast journalism. My Dad saw this as a romantic impulse stoked by broadcast journalists like Edward R. Murrow. Murrow's show *Person to Person* was viewed weekly on CBS in the Sikes household.

So, in 1976, as I left state government, I was given the opportunity to re-engage with my first love. Well, sort of.

I joined a friend, John Mahaffey, who had a group of radio stations in the Southwest. John brought me on as a (minor) partner with the intent to grow his business. As it turned out, I was not an especially good minor partner. I left after twelve months to start my own company. Fortunately a friend, Neal Ethridge, was willing to invest in my new enterprise.

The company I started bought and managed radio stations in Missouri and Colorado and did rather well. Two station combinations in Breckenridge, Colorado and Osage Beach, Missouri did especially well, making up for less prescient acquisitions in Springfield and Jackson, Missouri. Fortunately I had friends, led by Neal Ethridge, who were willing to invest in my acquisitions even though my experience was limited.

And then in 1985, after nine years building Sikes and Associates, I was once again tempted by Jack Danforth. Jack, as noted, helped open Secretary Baldrige's door on that cold December day.

# THE GORES: ALBERT AND TIPPER

*I am ashamed that until 1998 I didn't notice people.*

**Mikhail Khodorkovsky,
former imprisoned Russian oligarch**

In August of 1989, the US Senate, finishing its work before the summer recess, voted yea. I was confirmed to be the 24th Chairman of the Federal Communications Commission (FCC).

My work at the Commerce Department during President Reagan's Administration concentrated on domestic and international telecommunications trade, satellite and policy issues. This background proved to be very valuable in a rather complicated job during President George H. W. Bush's term. And once again, Jack Danforth helped close the sale. More on that later.

Late summers in Washington are hot, humid and disagreeable. In the Congress, there is always a legislative backlog paired with real or feigned urgency. In reality, most members of Congress want to go home and the ticking clock forces compromise. The nation's media then adds drama to legislative moves that precede a long recess. In the second decade of the 21$^{st}$ Century the drama is more often real, as the White House and Congress seem to represent different countries.

In my world, dealing with the legislative backlog was not just another rush for the exit. I was on the Senate calendar. It probably said "Alfred C. Sikes, nominee............pending confirmation."

But before delving into my strange and ultimately estranged relationship with Al Gore, a few words on my job in the Department of Commerce.

My time at Commerce was more revealing than productive. I did work with the White House on the elimination of the misnamed Fairness Doctrine.

I also gained a thorough indoctrination in international trade negotiations. America, having broken up AT&T, our dominant telecommunications company in 1984, was now open to foreign vendors of network and customer equipment. The break-up had required AT&T to sell off its equipment company, Western Electric.

The trade negotiating work, while interesting, barely moved the impenetrable wall which more nationalistic countries had erected to protect what they called their strategic industries. Their government leaders claimed that telecommunications was strategic and insisted, for the most part, on buying and using equipment made within their countries.

The only real exception was when US equipment was much better. In those instances, they imported our equipment and used it in state-owned or protected research and development to make sure they would over time become as technologically adept.

I am reminded of a conversation with the Deputy Trade Minister from South Korea during a trip to Seoul in 1988. We were talking over dinner about trade deficits and I recalled that the US had negotiated a voluntary export restraint agreement with Japan in 1981 that precluded their exporting more than 1.68 million automobiles to the US. The Trade Minister said, "We import Japanese cars." He added, "We buy one of each model." Obviously South Korea was using those imports as a part of their reverse-engineering research and development work.

So while I felt like I was getting a great education in

international economic competition, seeing many places in the world I hadn't visited as a mere civilian, I didn't feel particularly productive. Plus, the most important job at the National Telecommunications Administration was coordinating the use of radio frequencies by government agencies. Needless to say, the committee of agencies that oversaw that work had no interest in ideas that were more than modestly incremental. Fortunately, for me, much more interesting times were just ahead. I began to concentrate my time on the disruptive digital technologies and associated challenges that would tear at the Mid-20th Century fabric of communication's laws.

The weeks that preceded this last-minute flurry of legislative activity by the US Senate had brought to mind a pungent ten-second orientation on Washington that I had received forty-two months earlier. The Baldrige rule: "Everybody is after a piece of your ass. How do you rate yourself for aggressiveness?"

President George H. W. Bush nominated me to chair the FCC after his staff sorted through the various contenders and pretenders, floated trial balloons, and listened to various advocates lined up by the candidates and the special interest groups that worked to influence the FCC.

The detail of this political jockeying is old history, but suffice it to say I like to think my nomination occurred because of thoughtfulness, relevant credentials and integrity. *Wrong.*

While I cannot know with any precision why President Bush finally decided to nominate me, it didn't hurt to have Jack Danforth's strong support and the backing of the president's brother, Bucky Bush, a St. Louis banker and friend. Also President Bush's pollster, Bob Teeter, was a good friend and I had the active support of Kit Bond, Missouri's junior senator. Yet, while much of Washington conduct is predictable, the final run-up to my confirmation hearing was surprising, even bizarre.

When I arrived in Washington in 1986, Al Gore was a pivotal member of the Senate Commerce Committee. While the claim he had invented the Internet is patently false, he had been quite active in telecommunications policy. Gore was often quite farsighted. I had met with him a number of times, since my Commerce job was to help formulate telecommunications policy for President Reagan.

In one meeting, I had expressed admiration for his wife, Tipper Gore. She had led an effort some years earlier to shine an intense light on what were then called "blue lyrics" (no relationship to the Blues). Hard-rock lyrics frequently encouraged the use of drugs and glamorized sex without responsibility. Tipper Gore's work had resulted in my pulling some rock songs from a radio station I owned in the Cape Girardeau, Missouri media market. My program director was not amused.

Several weeks into the confirmation process, however, I received a rather jarring call. Senator Danforth's Chief-of-Staff Alex Netchvolodoff called to tell me that several ministers (to the extent they preached, it was in the corridors of power), who were active on indecent broadcasting issues in Washington, were going to testify against my confirmation and that Senator Gore was going to sponsor this panel of witnesses and oppose my confirmation.

This development seemed surreal—even in Washington. Since Gore's political party was in the majority, my confirmation was now at risk. Many nominees' aspirations fail because a single senator puts a hold on a confirmation vote. Senatorial courtesy is, I found, mostly limited to their relationships with their peers.

As the story unfolded, I learned that certain religious organizations were under the impression that then-candidate Bush had promised they would name Bush's FCC chair. I was not their candidate, so they decided to oppose me or, for that matter, even talk to me. Certitude leaves no room for curiosity. Their publicly stated reason for opposition was that I had been in the Reagan Administration, which had, in their view, been too libertarian.

They contacted Senator Gore, knowing that Senator Danforth foreclosed allies on the Republican side. Gore agreed to both sponsor a panel of witnesses that would oppose my candidacy and to vote against my confirmation. When the Committee voted me out with the recommendation I be confirmed, Gore put an anonymous hold on a vote by the whole Senate. So for several weeks nothing happened; I was stuck in Washington's version of a freeze frame.

Then as the August recess approached, Jack Danforth set up a meeting that had me waiting outside the Majority Leader

George Mitchell's office. He wanted Senator Mitchell to intervene and allow a confirmation vote before the recess.

The meeting with Mitchell was pivotal and went well. He was gracious and encouraging. The powerful should study his leadership technique; one of his enduring qualities was to appear to hold power with a light touch. Later that day he called Gore and told him to take his hold off or go public with it. Gore didn't want to go public with his explanation, so he removed the hold and I was confirmed the next day.

I had gotten to know the unfortunate side of Al Gore. He didn't hold, nor appear to hold, power with a light touch. Later in campaigns for vice president and president, he raised much of his money from Hollywood and recording industry moguls whose positions were antithetical to the position he took in my confirmation hearings. Hypocrisy is sometimes audacious. I guess his Hollywood allies overlooked this philosophical deviation as simply tactical.

The senator's life revolved around a singular ambition. He wanted to be president and was fully prepared to do whatever he could to buy favors. In his race for president, he lost his home state of Tennessee and thus the majority of the votes in the Electoral College. Those who know you best see opportunism first. Washington's power game is a hybrid of chess and a Middle Eastern rug market; not all the rugs are authentic.

• • •

I raised my hand that August day to be sworn in as the 24th Chairman of the FCC; I was once again painfully enlightened about the contortions of power and the extent to which personal motivations trump principles. I had survived a near-death experience. And in the closing years of the 20th Century, there were few places in Washington where the power game was more aggressively played. If action was your ticket, the FCC featured a lively game.

And I was on the cusp of a far more intimate understanding of the cultural undertow, the limits of government power and especially the beginnings of the digital revolution.

# SEX LEADS

*I wanted to create a kind of paradise, and it's a paradise closely associated with the idea of sexual freedom. But things have gone downhill. What we have now is consumer sex, and people are expected to have orgasms all the time. We're at this point. Where do we go from here?*

**French filmmaker, Alain Guiraudie**

*We need our imaginations, so diminished by millennia of idolatry and injustice, to be re-consecrated.*

**Andy Crouch, *Playing God***

Sex leads. Or violence. It's the Rupert Murdoch rule—although certainly not his alone. The contagion spread. Murdoch, the News Corporation mogul, understands appetites and the pull of tabloid news and its media derivatives. Profit is the primary test—maybe the only one.

My Washington days, in the early 1990s, were filled with minor and not so minor dramas. The impending digital revolution supplied much of the conflict as the major media companies fought to retain their position as gatekeepers. AT&T claimed it would be imperiled by the integration of another company's equipment on its phone network. If your company's assets were built around analog technology, the emergence of the far more robust digital technology seemed ominous.

Regardless of the importance of a range of issues dealing with technology and concentrated power, nothing is so preemptive as a drama with sex in the narrative. So while the FCC was working to shape the rules that would lead the digital revolution across telecommunications networks, sex talk by shock jocks on radio ended up commanding much of the public attention.

The issue was framed by complaints filed against the radio broadcaster that produced and aired *The Howard Stern Show*. Infinity Broadcasting was largely owned and led by profit-at-any-cost broadcaster, Mel Karmazin.

When I arrived at the FCC, I found that complaints against Stern's programs had piled up. The two chairmen I succeeded had a libertarian streak and were reluctant to take any action that might put the government in a position to impede free speech. When it came to the vulgar speech of Howard Stern, indulged by young boys, I didn't share their reluctance.

My view: the FCC was obligated to enforce the law aimed at protecting children from "indecent broadcasting," and as Arbitron ratings showed, young boys were a significant part of Stern's audience.

Now let me hit the pause button for a brief time and give you some necessary context. The indecent broadcasting law—then and today—extends only to TV and radio programs that are broadcast over the public airwaves and during the time of day children are likely to be in the audience. The law is intended to protect children from adults—not adults from each other. Today, of course, almost anything that is broadcast can be later accessed using the Internet.

So while in a sense the law is obsolete, the drama around its enforcement in the 1990s is instructive across a range of media today. And of course, the issue of how society treats its children is crucial and timeless.

Howard Stern was Mel Karmazin's meal ticket. Karmazin owned Infinity Broadcasting and the nationwide distribution of Stern's show gave Infinity a lucrative inventory of advertisers who wanted to reach boys and young men with their pitches.

The backup of complaints against Stern resulted in part from a man in Los Angeles who taped each one of Stern's morning shows and filed formal complaints against many of his vulgar routines. Karmazin did not want the FCC to begin a proceeding on the complaints, so he came in to see me several times after he concluded that I was seriously considering taking action.

In one meeting I asked Karmazin whether he had any printed policies on what disc jockeys could say over the air. Karmazin quickly said no, and went on to explain that such policies would restrain Stern's spontaneity and creativity. I can't say that I was surprised, even though it was common practice in the industry to have some policies on dos and don'ts along with time delay mechanisms. The licensed broadcaster was responsible for what went out over the air.

I decided to work through the backlog and reach a decision on whether the complaints were actionable. I asked each FCC commissioner to appoint a legal aide to a Commission Task Force so that we could act in unison.

Forty-five days later, the task force, having finished reviewing the Stern show transcripts, recommended that the Commission consider as actionable three of Stern's routines out of the dozens submitted. Stern's routines, by the way, weren't the only ones examined. He might have been the most notorious, but in the sordid world of shock jocks, imitation was rife.

It is also important to note that then and now, all this pushing and shoving over minor restrictions to protect children follows a predictable script. Much of the media—and certainly all Hollywood—characterize any effort to moderate radio or TV or any medium's content as censorious and perforce bad. Keeping in mind that the only legal efforts are to protect children, this story line is in serious need of re-examination. Nurturing—not abusing—children should always be a tier-one consideration.

FCC historians and communications lawyers might have an interest in the legal and procedural detail. I will spare you. But one important detail should not be left out.

Most FCC decisions reached after aggressive advocacy are appealed. In what I will call the Stern cases, Infinity Broadcasting appealed, hoping at the very least to buy some time during which Stern could continue his shtick unrestrained. And in the context of Infinity's earnings, Karmazin saw just over a million dollars in fines as little more than a nuisance.

At one point I suggested to several commissioners that we might want to move from fines to consideration of license revocation. I knew that would get Karmazin's attention. But given the Commission's history with RKO General broadcast licenses in the 1970s and '80s, that was further than the commissioners wanted to go, especially Jim Quello. In the RKO case, a challenge to one of its TV licenses spread to all of its twenty or so radio and TV stations. Essentially the Commission, and subsequently the courts, determined that if RKO General did not have the requisite character to hold one license, it didn't have the right to hold the others.

I understood their reluctance. If the Commission had begun a proceeding on Infinity's Los Angeles station from which the complaints against the Stern sex stuff began, that action would effectively put all of Infinity's broadcast licenses at legal risk. Regardless of my frustration with Karmazin's intransigence, that was further than I wanted to go.

Eventually Karmazin sought to merge Infinity with CBS, and CBS required that Karmazin resolve his FCC disputes. The fines were then paid.

When I became FCC Chairman, many believed the FCC to be their only recourse in the cultural assault. Today, comparatively, the FCC's power is decidedly secondary to the power of devices and software and networks. My thesis: the power of the Internet in all of its many facets should be used and is being used as a cultural corrective.

While President Obama was using advanced targeting to reach and organize his constituency, revolutionaries in the less developed world were using the same tools to effect revolutions. Twitter and Facebook were pivotal tools in Egypt and the Ukraine. Iranian autocrats and North Korea's latest Kim attack the Internet much as their predecessors attacked radio and TV.

Ultimately, they will lose.

The fact is profound change in thought leadership will likely be led by grassroots leaders using leading edge tools. Rarely are business or government leaders conscious culture shapers—profit and reelection organize their thoughts and motivate their actions.

If more benign leadership becomes media leadership, purchase boycotts will have been the vehicle. Financial pain will have to occur; otherwise the lowest common denominator will continue to prevail across much of the media spectrum—the race to the bottom will continue. On the hopeful side, at no other time have the tools to counter this force been more powerful.

While I was FCC Chairman, Infinity Broadcasting was fined over a million dollars due to Stern routines, but it was not until two years after I arrived in New York that Infinity paid the FCC fines. Eventually, Stern left broadcast radio and became a part of subscription radio on Sirius. He also has a television gig as one of several judges on *America's Got Talent*. Fortunately this TV gig doesn't offer him an opportunity to use incest and masturbation narratives.

The FCC actions pushed Stern even further into the spotlight and then out of it, at least for a time. He faded from the national conversation, as he had to take his shtick to pay radio.

Between the initial action in late 1989 and its affirmation in 1996, I became part of Stern's daily radio routine. His 1992 attack was particularly noteworthy. In October of that year I had prostate cancer surgery, a fact that was in the news. On Stern's show the day the report broke, he told his listeners he hoped I would die in the hospital. In late 2005, in response to *60 Minutes* Ed Bradley, he said he had some regret about that attack, but would probably do it again.

By the summer of 1994, I was living and working in New York City, when a call came in from the general counsel of the FCC. He asked if I minded if he gave my phone number to a lawyer who was trying to settle the estate of a woman who had made me her beneficiary. I was puzzled. Did I have some long-lost relative, a rich aunt that my parents had never mentioned? And why would the contact come through the FCC? A small mystery, an intriguing call; "Sure," I said, "have him give me a call."

Later that day the picture in the puzzle pieces began to

emerge. I had become the heir to the estate of a Shrewsbury, Massachusetts librarian who had specifically eliminated the names of the previous heirs—her sisters—on her pension form and substituted me. My name was entered as "Alfred C. Sikes, Chairman of the FCC." A bit more research dated her change of beneficiary back to the time Stern and I were paired in the news. Our antagonisms had been a regular part of the news for some time, so my name and positions were rather well known.

It is, of course, impossible for me to put myself in her mind. But I can imagine. Perhaps more than any, librarians understand the importance of words—their invisible power. Words have sway; they alter minds. Librarians devote themselves to organizing them and helping others find their best works. The librarian from Shrewsbury understood that Stern was more than just a foul-mouthed shock jock cracking vulgar jokes on radio. She understood the power of his words—particularly on young minds.

She understood, implicitly, that the powerful business forces that were using shock jocks were assaulting and inevitably coarsening our culture. They were steepening the downhill slope.

The estate was principally her pension, which had a cash value of about $15,000. The estate lawyer wanted me to waive my claim so that her three sisters would receive the proceeds. I did.

I recognize, of course, that conventional radio—Stern's initial medium—has been overtaken. In some ways we might wish for a world where the greatest danger to immature minds is listening to vulgar shock jocks on the radio. However, we are now in a world that led Holly Finn, in a *Wall Street Journal* article on online pornography, to reflect: "Imagine seeing *Last Tango in Paris* before your first kiss."

But this fact does not change the overriding lesson of the Shrewsbury librarian. Words and images are powerful, and their use in any setting where young minds are being formed should be done with consideration shaped by discretion and informed by character.

In many ways, however, the more serious problem is business leadership without character—the elimination of community implications in the cost-benefit analysis. Upstream of Stern was Mel Karmazin, who had an unerring eye for the lowest common denominator. He led the race to the bottom. Karmazin had one measure—profit margin.

I was reminded recently of Karmazin while reading about the World Wrestling Entertainment (WWE) network. Its founder, Vince McMahon, was interviewed for an article in *Forbes* (April 14, 2014), which began by citing WWE's success.

McMahon, noting a mounted dinosaur skull in his office quipped, "When you feed the monster, the monster is happy. The problem with that is the monster grows. And as the monster grows, then the monster wants more to eat. And as long as you do that, everything's great. And if you don't provide the food, then bad things start to happen."

The reporter asks, "Is the monster the audience?"

"You can look at it that way, absolutely," McMahon says with a smile. Presumably the bad thing is less profit.

WWE is a combustible mix of violence, sex and misogyny. And to feed the monster (the audience), WWE dials up its outrages.

WWE manifests many aspects of the popular culture. It is led by a man with an unerring eye for exploiting human weakness. It is all appetite and no soul. McMahon scripts decadence. But as he conceded, the audience (monster) has to be fed escalating violence, sex and misogyny.

A story well told causes us to suspend our disbelief—we are swept up into the storyteller's world.

In untold ways, the stories we tell—through music, movies, books, video games, advertisements and the like—shape society. Tyrants know this; it is why in much of the world, stories are censored.

We all feel the pressure. I cringe when perfect smile ads come on. A mix of injury and inadequate orthodontics have robbed me of the perfect smile. I can imagine the pressure on immature minds as advertisers and their Madison Avenue collaborators work on their self-image to sell fashions, cosmetics, alcohol, relationships, and the like.

The United States Constitution provides its storytellers the most comprehensive, yet simply expressed guarantee of freedom in the history of mankind. It, the right to free expression, is at the heart of a healthy democracy.

And at the heart of an unhealthy democracy are people like Mel Karmazin and Vince McMahon who coarsen the culture and ultimately limit societies' freedom; as the collective, we respond to the resulting pathologies with ever more government. We need to keep in mind that government and money are not antidotes to poison.

# CHILDREN

*What's celebrity sex, Dad?" It was my 7-year-old son, who had been looking over my shoulder at my computer screen. He mispronounced "celebrity" but spoke the word "sex" as if he had been using it all his life. "Celebrity six," I said, abruptly closing my AOL screen, "it's a game famous people play in teams of three," I said, as I ushered him out of my office and downstairs into what I assumed was the safety of the living room.*

**Lee Siegel, New York writer and critic**

*When Hollywood wants to discourage cigarette smoking it knows exactly how to do it, because it knows exactly how much power it has to deliver cultural messages.*

**Author Peggy Noonan**

*Adult life begins in a child's imagination, and we've relinquished that imagination to the marketplace.*

**Dana Gioia, American poet and writer**

Hillary Clinton wrote a book titled *It Takes a Village.*

Ms. Clinton's theme was that while parents have the primary responsibility of childrearing, their children are going to be shaped, at least in part, by the culture.

Perverse culture; trouble ahead.

Parents have always needed the village, but never as much as today. My parents, living in a small town far away from television towers, didn't buy a TV until I was in high school. My dad was not going to spend money to pull in snowy images from television stations more than a hundred miles away in either St. Louis or Memphis. Electronic devices, with their promise of distraction and pleasure, didn't exist.

Perhaps most importantly, the nation's creative leaders—the storytellers—had a sense of responsibility—and yes, there were network censors. So whether the stories were in song lyrics, TV shows or books, they reflected a more benign, nurturing civilization, one shaped, in part, by values that most believed to be transcendent. The village, for the most part, treated children as precious and vulnerable.

But the village has changed. And when the conversation turns to media aimed at tweens and teens, few find emotional or intellectual comfort, much less hope. Parents hope the apologetic sociologists are right when they conclude that this too will pass.

Most uncomfortably, in this decade, mass shootings have all too frequently commanded the news and attacked the collective nervous system. Columbine—Eric Harris and Dylan Klebold; Newtown—Adam Lange; Virginia Tech—Seung-Hui Cho; Aurora—James Holmes; Tucson—Jared Loughner; Charleston—Dylann Roof. Lone Male shooters emptying their gun's magazines on the innocent. Mass shootings have gone from rare to occasional to ordinary.

After each mass killing, we try to make sense of what happened. Rarely do we. Inevitably the lone shooters are portrayed as mentally ill. After all, this diagnosis relieves us of any responsibility; all civilizations have had to deal with the mentally ill, we tell ourselves. It's easier to isolate a human being and pronounce him mentally ill than it is to take a hard look at the illness in our culture and try to do something about it.

Supreme Court Justice Oliver Wendell Holmes Jr. famously observed in *Schenck v. United States* that falsely shouting "Fire" in a crowded theater is not protected by the First Amendment's guarantee of free speech. Holmes found nothing redemptive in that: it was all costs, no benefits.

There is an implicit recognition that media content is culturally important and not value-free. So we rate films, video games and the like. Ratings then become a version of the hidden fruit. Young people find hidden fruit impossible to resist and are particularly inventive when it comes to opening the electronic window. Parents often turn to their children to find out how to access a movie without having to buy overburdened and costly cable or satellite television packages.

The "fire in the theater" case is easy. A number of less cerebral justices would have reached the same conclusion. But when it comes to salacious narratives and companion stimulation, they are always said to be artistic and thus protected. A video game that tests the killing quickness of a player gets wrapped into a faux narrative. And since violent and obscene behavior is part of life, there is always the *artistic-value* defense.

Civilization has generally treated young minds as fragile. Certainly, in my personal experience, there has always been an invisible line when it comes to adult relationships with children and youth. And of course, children become adults, and we all know that our early experiences in childhood follow us through life. As the poet Dana Gioia noted, "Adult life begins in a child's imagination, and we've relinquished that imagination to the marketplace."

The power of this invisible line has been an essential element in our nation's historical strength. It has centered our civilization. It has protected the most vulnerable from others and themselves. It has been a part of the moral tone of our nation and has helped set and sustain it. But now, and for some time, it has been under constant attack. In dealing with the combustible subjects of violence and sex, it has almost disappeared.

*The Economist* magazine, capitalizing on the branding of generations, titled an opinion piece Generation XXX noting, "Because of smartphones, tablets and laptops, hardcore material can be accessed privately by anyone. The result is that many teenagers today have seen a greater number and variety of sex acts than the most debauched Mughal emperor managed in a lifetime."

Howard Stern saw the threshold on human default settings move in his own family. I suspect he had at least some hope that modesty would influence the roles his daughter accepted in her theatrical career. But the line had moved. News reports said he was livid.

His then twenty-two-year-old daughter, Emily, played pop star Madonna in *Kabbalah*, an Off-Broadway satire. She played the final ten minutes nude. After a talk with her father, she pulled out of the play.

Stern's actions punctuate Reinhold Niebuhr's assessment of human weakness. Niebuhr, a philosopher and theologian, observed that individual humans are more moral than groups of humans. Moral father—immoral entertainer.

It is hard to know whether a line, informed by Judeo-Christian values, even exists in commercial decision making. A significant part of our entertainment, especially that which is aimed at the young, is based more on stimulation than storytelling. And it is clear that yesterday's stimulative episode will just not do. Yesterday's stimulation is predictable, boring, unimaginative. When gratuitous violence or sex trumps narrative, escalation is inevitable. To sustain an audience, violence has to become more violent, sex more erotic or bizarre, outrage yet more outrageous.

The powerful, through much of our history, largely honored the line of propriety separating youth from adults; transcendent values or a strong intuitive or inherited sense of right and wrong defined discretion. Today, however, many of the power elite honor only those lines drawn by felony laws.

When debasement is the content, there should be an editor, or ultimately a business leader, who weighs the consequences. And when it comes to content that targets children and youth, the ultimate question should be, "Do I want my children and their friends to be fed a diet of this content?" We live in a cacophonous age and everything that is produced is imitated ad nauseam—small streams quickly become rivers. It is also eventually available around the clock on any networked device— the village writ large. Indeed, there is no longer a village, just a largely value-free electronic cacophony.

If James Madison, the principal author of the Bill of Rights, were crafting an article on speech protection today, I believe the constitutional line would be somewhat different. Political speech and virtually all material written or produced for mature people would be no less protected. Indecent broadcasting and gratuitous violence aimed at the immature? I am not so sure.

America's deepest thinkers, I believe, would have made it clear that words and images that both target children and violate them would receive scrutiny and face a test of propriety. It hardly takes a deep thinker to understand that society should protect children.

Each day's news, frequently about excess, is instructive. Adults in large numbers fall victim to the "eat more, drink more, buy more, screw more" themes of pop culture and advertising. At least adults have had a sufficient number of years to form their values or at least weigh risks and rewards. Not true of children.

John-Paul Sartre, the French philosopher and writer wrote of our being "condemned to freedom." I am reminded of a bit of humor in a single newspaper comic panel. It showed two goldfish in a bowl with one talking, the other listening. The talkative one said, "The people outside aren't really free. They just have a bigger bowl." Sound familiar?

The cartoonist captured the view of German philosopher Georg Wilhelm Friedrich Hegel, who believed that "no man can surpass his own time, for the spirit of his time is also his own spirit."

As Liam Stack of the *New York Times* (December 31, 2015) reported: Famed filmmaker, George Lucas, the creator of *Star Wars*, in an interview with Charlie Rose said filmmakers in the Soviet Union had more freedom then their counterparts in Hollywood, who, he maintained, "have to adhere to a very narrow line of commercialism." He summed up: "profit over storytelling."

Are we locked into the spirit of our time until some cataclysmic event forces a new spirit? Are we inured to cataclysmic events? Is there a chance to break free and reset our direction?

• • •

When I arrived in New York in 1993, Times Square was saturated with sex shops and their clientele. A year or so later the newly minted mayor, Rudy Giuliani, vowed to clean up Times Square and gathered politicians from various parties and points of view in a bipartisan movement.

The fight to clean up Times Square was not without contention. The sex shop owners claimed their right to free speech was being regulated out of existence. And while this charge might not receive a friendly reaction in Oklahoma City, New Yorkers take all manner of speech seriously.

There is, of course, a whole body of case law on the extent to which municipalities can use their regulatory authority to restrict sex shops. Also, a pedestrian will not be stopped if he wants to use his smartphone to go to a hard core pornography Web site while at 42$^{nd}$ and 8$^{th}$ Avenue in Manhattan. But the atmosphere along the streets where we live, work and play is important in shaping our culture. New York's leadership knew that Times Square needed to be more than an adult shopping experience writ large.

Regulatory authority was used as a counterforce to clean up Times Square and a favorable tipping point was reached. Increasingly, however, the tipping point of cultural regeneration will have to be triggered by concerned citizens pushing back. Our constitutional right to free speech knows only rare limits.

As the sleazy side of Times Square diminished, tourism began to flourish and businesses to serve the continual flow of domestic and international visitors increased. Today, Times Square is vibrant, successful and, by most measures, vastly better.

There was a time, not so long ago, when a large percentage of the transitory population of Times Square was there to hurt people. Now people who go to see Broadway or the overwhelming blend of outsized electronic signs or street musicians or just each other—indeed the Big Apple scene—feel safe.

At various moments in my lifetime the cultural trajectory has been uphill. We were led by mountain climbers like Martin Luther King, Jr., whose dreams looked well beyond the horizon. His dreams helped shape the culture and then, to a large degree, became it. And perhaps to the embarrassment of those who attack faith in God, his dreams and actions were inspired by and explicitly integrated with his faith. His movement began in the churches.

King hasn't been the only mountain climber, but few others have influenced the culture more profoundly. King was climbing the same mountain that Lincoln had generations earlier. Both were assassinated.

Lincoln's career began in Vandalia, Illinois, which was briefly the state's capital. Today Vandalia's largest employer is the Vandalia Correction Center. The average age in this male-only prison is thirty. How did we let that happen?

We follow the slope while always hoping. We frequently say that our nation's future will turn on the promise of the younger generation. But if we are honest, then we are concerned. What happens when public education fails so many? What happens when a significant number of parents are so self-regarding that there is little time for their children? What happens when license becomes licentiousness? What happens when children become prey? What happens when prisons become a leading employer? It can't be good.

# ON FREE SPEECH

*But what divides Estonians and Russians most is their media. Those whose mother tongue is Russian rely largely on news from Russian state media. Its worldview has rubbed off. Researchers at the Sinu Riigi Kaitse programme, who study young ethnic Russians, find a sharp worsening of attitudes toward America and NATO.*

**The Economist, March 7, 2015**

*It would not have been possible for us to take power or to use it in the ways we have without the radio.*

**Joseph Goebbels, Hitler's Minister of Propaganda**

In 1986, I renewed an acquaintance with Clarence Thomas, then chairman of the Equal Opportunity Employment Commission (EEOC). While Clarence and I had both been in Jack Danforth's Attorney General Office in Jefferson City, Missouri, by the time he arrived, I had moved on.

At the time of our Washington meeting I had just started working for Mac Baldrige at the Commerce Department leading the National Telecommunications and Information Administration. I was hoping that Clarence might be a friendly counselor—I had a few friends who worked on Capitol Hill, but almost no friends who worked in the Executive Branch. An Ivy League education often resulted in a network of Washington friends; I didn't have one. Most of my friends were still in my home state.

Clarence and I shared several lunches over the next few years. We were unguarded in a town where most relationships are freighted with conflicting ambitions. Clarence provided me excellent insights, and most importantly, after I was nominated to chair the FCC, he recommended his managing director at EEOC, Andy Fishel, to become my managing director. Andy became a key part of my team.

It is hard for me to overstate my shock when, in July of 1991, after Thomas was nominated by President George H.W. Bush to serve on the US Supreme Court, he was charged with sexual harassment by Anita Hill, then a professor at the law school at Oklahoma University.

I was at the FCC when Thomas characterized the US Senate confirmation process as a "high-tech lynching of uppity blacks." The gavel-to-gavel televised hearings of the Senate Judiciary Committee were a magnet for viewers complaints and letters to me. Clarence was suddenly vaulted from being a rather low-profile government official into being a household name, whose character was being, in part, defined by those who would do anything to block his confirmation. It is hard to imagine a more combustible mix—power, judicial philosophy, race, sex, and partisanship, all blended into a high-stakes political showdown. Novelists were envious. Thomas ended up being confirmed by a 52 to 48 vote after sensational and, for Clarence, destructive hearings. He began the hearings with a good reputation and ended it with his character tarnished.

My job at the FCC carried with it a false impression. Many thought that the FCC could somehow intervene and restrict speech. Over and over complaints arrived at our doorstep about news coverage; the coverage over the Thomas affair was certainly not an exception. We had a boilerplate response—political speech was free unless it was untruthful, and in the case of public figures, malicious, and in that case, the courts provided the only remedy. Charges of libel or slander had to begin with a petition filed with a court clerk.

Regardless of what I thought about the fairness of the attacks on my friend, it was clear that America's promise of free speech would result in the most comprehensive coverage imaginable. Inevitably however, power politics, when mixed with incendiary accusations, are ugly and the press needs to avoid being swept up into a particular narrative. But—and this is the important point—the fairness of the coverage is not for the government to determine.

• • •

In 1991, I had a far different exposure to speech and power. I was asked by the White House to take America's principle of free speech to Romania, Hungary, and Czechoslovakia. Each had been freed from Soviet domination by homegrown revolution as the Soviet Union was collapsing. Each was facing the challenge of building civil institutions that would protect the citizenry from a return to tyrannical power. As I met with government officials, journalists and academics it became clear that America's rock-hard devotion to free speech was puzzling, if not threatening, to many. Case in point: I can vividly remember a shouting match I started in a meeting in Bucharest, Romania, as journalists and academics fought to get the microphone so they could have the next or last word.

My trip to Romania mainly involved trying to persuade government officials that they should enact laws to encourage private ownership of TV and radio stations. I also encouraged the enactment of a home-grown version of our constitutional guarantee of free speech. President H. W. Bush believed that this combination would assure an effective check on government power. We spoke about it on the eve of my trip.

We decided that I should also ask for a meeting with those who had been dissidents during the Ceausescu regime. Nicolae Ceausescu had been head of the Romanian Communist Party and head of state for over twenty years and was a Stalinist in his iron-fisted rule. My question to the dozens who attended was simple. I began by explaining the importance of the First Amendment to the US Constitution and then asked what they thought about such an addition to their constitutional rewrite, which was in progress.

Essentially they used the threat of pornography rhetorically. Free speech, many said, "would be abused by pornographers." But as the shouting match ripened, it was clear that a number of otherwise thoughtful people simply didn't want contrary views to have the same constitutional status as theirs. Dissent, they were saying, is all right if it is constrained.

Often when my role became a diplomatic one—principally when I represented the US government in international meetings—discomfort ensued. I tend to be fairly plainspoken and somewhat impatient to get to the heart of what I see as a problem. Diplomats, on the other hand, specialize in politeness or, if they don't want to resolve an issue, evasive politeness. What I found in Bucharest in talking to the dissidents was a hyper-emotional response, certainly well outside of diplomatic exchange, over what is a very profound question. When should speech not be free? Interestingly in the US today that question often surrounds the circumvention of free speech where it should find fertile ground—in colleges and universities.

I got another dose of this allergy to criticism from no less a democrat than President Jimmy Carter. In 1990, I joined an initiative that the former president and Mikhail Gorbachev began—to engage Soviet officials on the subject of independent broadcasting in what I thought of as a post-dictatorial world. At that point, the Soviet government and its former satellites owned all the broadcast stations, TV and radio alike. Again, the central theme was the importance of free speech in electronic media in sustaining democratic institutions.

At a meeting in Saint Petersburg, Russia, there was a very telling exchange. By the time this meeting took place in 1994, the Soviet Union had collapsed and our conferees included both Russian broadcasters and government officials and those from the former Warsaw Bloc countries. The latter, in the now amended Commission name, were called *Independent States*.

The meeting in Saint Petersburg took place in a luxurious

hotel conference center and, if memory serves, there were several dozen of us arrayed around a circular table with a placard noting our official position.

President Carter chaired the discussion, which quickly featured free speech criticisms that were earnest, predictable, and wrong. Many from the former Soviet Union said the only way they could build a healthy government was if the loud-mouthed critics were silenced. They had no experience with free speech and were certain that giving all sides, regardless of merit, an uncensored voice would undermine their efforts.

President Carter, I presume preferring to appear sympathetic, voiced his own painful experience with television and radio critics and noted that in America each broadcaster received a license to do business from the FCC and it was for a term of years and had to be renewed. He then stated, "that the license term was seven years and perhaps it should be only three years, so the government could make sure the privilege of being a broadcaster was not abused."

Up to that point President Carter and I had enjoyed a collegial relationship—or at least I had. I certainly had gone out of my way to respect him for both forming the commission and, of course, his service as President. Now, however, I could not keep my mouth shut. I quickly responded, noting that if the government had a frequent right to deny license renewal, not only would the right of free speech be undermined, but that broadcasters in the private sector would not invest in facilities and programs with uncertainty about continued ownership.

The President's endearing smile disappeared and our collegial relationship ended.

• • •

On a more personal level, when I bought my first radio station in Breckenridge, I valued the fact that KLGT was the only daily news source across Summit County, Colorado. So, while KLGT was just a single station in a small town, the traditions of broadcast responsibility, originating with this nation's founding documents, were clearly on my mind.

When you own the sole daily news medium, you necessarily engage the question of fairness. Your listeners demand it. While the news director at KLGT had a small audience, he had a big megaphone. I expect my attitude of balance and fairness was shared by most small town station owners and managers.

Today's world of digital networks and devices literally gives anybody who chooses to engage in the national conversation a chance to become a part of the news media. We certainly don't have too little speech; we have too much speech that is biased, underinformed, superficial, and, at times, angry.

Perversely, the exercise of free speech in America too frequently undermines its profound position. According to Gallup survey work in 2012, 60 percent of the public has little or no confidence in the news. When our eyes and ears and translators are not trusted, the country's health is in decline.

In many ways, news coverage today goes back to the cultural leadership question: Who is leading, the media owner or the perceived necessity to feed the voracious appetite of popular culture?

Rupert Murdoch's influence has accentuated fault lines in the news. Murdoch has certainly been a seminal media leader over the last twenty-five years.

He has spoken disparagingly about "eat your vegetables" news coverage. His essential point: news needs to entertain— not just inform. My view: important issues must be covered whether they are entertaining or not, and news directors need to find ways to interest the public while providing necessary information.

A United Kingdom freelance writer WD Fyfe had a biting, but amusing, take on Murdoch-styled journalism after his UK paper, *News of the World*, was found to have hacked into the phone calls of crime victims. Fyfe said that journalists were constantly rating films and the like and proposed a rating system for news outlets:

*The problem is, how would you rate them? Like fast food: sleazy, extra sleazy and super-sleaze-me? Or maybe like movies, except instead of stars, we could use buckets of slime? That way we could talk about three and four slime journalism. Or perhaps we could just use an inverted triangle with Rupert Murdoch upside down at the bottom and the rest of them clawing their way down to get there. Personally, I like a straight number system; International Murdoch Units. For example, a newspaper that hacks the phone records of teenage murder victims could be assigned 100 International Murdochs. A television network that convicts a lacrosse team of rape— without any evidence—could be given 99.5 Murdochs. Radio stations that blather on about President Obama's birth certificate could be given 99 units and so on and so forth. Journalists themselves could also be assigned numbers starting with Rebekah Brooks who could be 100 Murdochs, Nancy Grace could be 99.999 and guys like Glenn Beck 106. Then a simple formula of accumulated International Murdoch Units divided by the journalist's own Murdoch Number would reveal just how sleazy each media outlet is. Eventually, we news consumers could get a pretty clear picture, and we could adjust our reading, viewing and listening habits accordingly.*

Of course Mr. Fyfe does not sermonize on who are the "we"— the raters. In today's hyper-partisan environment, it would be impossible to find disinterested parties. On the other, hand we should pay attention to the more global view of the media—as noted in public opinion survey after survey, it is not good.

To be fair, the deterioration of news coverage is a complex affair, but the lowest common denominator business model often frames the underlying issues. Certainly some of Murdoch's holdings, the *Wall Street Journal* for example, are good journalistic enterprises. Fox News provides a valuable counterforce to what previously had too often been a follow-the-leader—*New York Times*—news pack. Increasingly over the last two decades, however, more and more time and space are devoted to soft news or what some call infotainment.

*New York Times* columnist Maureen Dowd weighed in on February 7, 2015 after NBC anchor, Brian Williams, was suspended for embellishing his personal risk while covering the Iraq war:

*TV news now is rife with cat, dog and baby videos, weather stories and narcissism. And even that fare*

*caused trouble for Williams when he reported on a video*
*of a pig saving a baby goat, admitting "we have no way*
*of knowing if it's real," and then later had to explain that*
*it wasn't. The nightly news anchors are not figures of*
*authority. They're part of the entertainment, branding*
*and cross-promotion business.*

There is, of course, nothing wrong with stories about celebrities or animals or movies or a long list of our amusements. There are certainly a number of shows with those themes. But today in a twenty-minute network news segment, known as the *network* news, those stories consume more than half the time.

According to Pew Research, approximately 22 million people view the network's news shows; the serious news void is not inconsequential. Since around 140 million watch what Nielsen calls live TV, the fact that somewhat less than 15 percent watch the network news should enlighten those who run the network news divisions. Perhaps more robust coverage of hard news would attract more listeners while giving their news divisions some sense of accomplishment.

Today cable news networks, even with their baked-in biases—the most popular being Rupert Murdoch and Roger Ailes's Fox News—provide more hard news. But when you watch these newscasts, it is evident most of the viewers are older. The newscasts are surrounded by health care advertisements of one sort or another.

We also face a civilization question. If we principally get our news from hard-edged and often partisan sources, can public debate remain civil? Increasingly my experience is that fewer and fewer people are comfortable with discussions about current events. Cable news networks have defined a right-left divide that is often filled with angry rhetoric. I can recall more than a few dinner parties when discussing some current event rapidly devolved into stridency and hurt feelings. Too bad.

It is, of course, certain that debate over important subjects is not for the weak-hearted—or minded. Thomas Jefferson, James Madison, John Adams and Alexander Hamilton wrote or retained writers to pen hard-edged attacks on their opponents. But at least the ebb and flow of their rhetoric was mostly about ideas.

Now, disinterested persons are not going to suddenly become interested simply because news coverage improves, but that is not an excuse for lowest common denominator journalism. America needs journalistic leadership, including business owners, who understand their privileged positions come with obligation. They need to find comfortable business models, learn to make important issues interesting, and avoid entrapment by race-to-the-bottom narratives.

Fox News has probably sought to trademark "fair and balanced and unafraid"—this is its branding slogan, which its on-air personalities repeat often. I watch Chris Wallace's show on Sunday and believe it is mostly "fair and balanced and unafraid." And Fox news segments dealing with issues that do not attract right/left polarity are often the same.

I mention Fox News because a recent Quinnipiac Poll found that 29 percent regarded Fox as the most trusted network. CNN followed at 22 percent, CBS and NBC registered 10 percent and MSNBC trailed the field at 7 percent. Republicans were more likely to find favor with Fox and Democrats with CNN. And Fox News having drawn over 24 million viewers for the first Republican debate—thanks to Donald Trump—is now in an even stronger position.

MSNBC, which received the worst rating, is owned by Comcast, which also owns NBC. It is a huge company that in 2014 generated over $8 billion in free cash flow. Free cash flow is cash available for business investment. Given the abysmal ratings of its cable news network—MSNBC—NBC should have the journalistic and business mission of living up to Fox's branding claim—with one addition. My recommendation: *Fair, Balanced, Unafraid and Trusted.* I understand that self-proclamation of trustworthiness is high-risk, but if a news network lived up to that motto, their audience would confirm the reality. With my business hat on, I know a strong audience position will not be easily or quickly accomplished. But it's doable, worth the risk and something Brian Roberts, CEO of Comcast, might aspire to have recognized in his obituary.

Books take a while to get published. Publishers, understandably, want to check them for facts and edit them for clarity. So, by the time you read this riff on free speech and media standards, the world will have moved on. But since innumerable embarrassments and negative polls seem to fall on deaf ears, my guess is that the issue of a well-informed citizenry will not have disappeared.

# IMPROVISATION

*Beethoven's music comes from agrarian culture, addressing a monarchy, that type of a political situation, and Duke Ellington's music deals with democracy and a technological culture.*

**Wynton Marsalis, trumpeter**

*The success of jazz is a victory for democracy, and a symbol of the aesthetic dignity, which is finally spiritual, that performers can achieve and express as they go about inventing music and meeting the challenge of the moment.*

**Stanley Crouch, music and cultural critic**

In the last few years I have been to several concerts headlined by very talented musicians. And for the most part, their concert repertoire was at least a generation old—indeed, their fans demanded it.

One particularly vivid memory is of standing with hundreds of enthusiastic, indeed slightly crazed fans, while we all sang along with Don McLean, who penned the music and lyrics to America's rock anthem, *American Pie*.

Musical tributes, reunion tours, and the like return us to our youth and its hopeful emotions and passionate loves. They return us to an earlier groove that our blurred memory perceives to have been more comfortable.

But jazz is both America's gift to the world and helps define its exceptionalism. Earlier and timeless melodies are replayed, if sometimes in faint recollection, and then improvisation allows gifted artists to take us on a new journey. Tributes are paid to Ellington and Armstrong and Brubeck, but even the best-known songs are not frozen in time. Improvisation happens.

Washington is mostly frozen in time. Political talking points have become as familiar as lyrics from a generation or more ago. And regardless of how this or that program is spelled out, too often debt remains the lubricant for promises while the tax code looks like insects preserved in an outsized piece of amber.

Washington lyricists come and go, but the underlying music does not change. The political parties are mostly in a time warp, framed by aggressively enforced orthodoxies guarded by hyper-aggressive interest groups. No jazz there—indeed, no music at all.

The public can hear the stale discord and their frustration is palpable. Crucially important institutions barely register on the approval end of the scale. Gallup recently asked a representative sample of citizens about a range of institutions and asked each respondent whether they had a "great deal" of confidence in the institution. The presidency, Congress and the news media each registered less than 15 percent.

What happens to a country when confidence sinks so low? What happens when the institutions, given leadership responsibility by the Constitution, become the butt of dark humor, not just satire? What happens when the institution that enjoys free speech protection loses the faith of its presumed beneficiaries? Is this ominous or simply cyclical?

In Washington, power is the currency and defines the culture. Most frequently, it translates into how much money a given politician or bureaucrat has to spend. Money buys things and thus confers at least a perception of power. Since we are egregiously sloppy when it comes to measuring outcomes, the overarching political value is money—appropriations, not outcomes.

A case in point, from my own experience. Few know that the FCC levies taxes. The taxes show up on your phone bill as additional charges and are used to help underwrite universal telecommunications service. For decades the dollars were used to subsidize phone rates in high-cost areas, more often than not defined by a lack of population density. Today the FCC concentrates on the spread of high-speed data service and spends four times what was spent in the early to mid-nineties— taxation without representation.

The FCC has managed to flip the price-benefit model. Technology has turned the smartphone into a super-computer, while compression technologies and fiber optics have dramatically lowered the cost per bit of information transmitted. Yet as the relative cost of computer and transmission power has dropped, FCC expenditures have quadrupled.

And of course, those who apply the lobbying pressure for the FCC to spend more and more, are, in significant part, funded by those who sell the equipment and services.

This, unfortunately, is not a revelation. We all know the growth in government spending has outpaced the federal government's capacity to make a positive contribution to our collective lives. The dissonance—and not the musical variety— is amplified every day in our lives. And what we know works perversely on the body politic. We become untrusting, if not cynical. We intuitively calculate that we can't really influence the larger picture, so we will just look after ourselves, and then we rate unfavorably the pillars of our freedom. The enablers, the big business and labor organizations that often underwrite those in charge, are viewed no more favorably.

Along the way, what really began to gnaw on me was the imbalance of talent and motivation; frequently the most talented advocates worked for embedded interests that enjoyed government favors. There was more heft outside the buildings of government than inside them.

Part of my job, as I saw it, was enabling new and promising technologies. Obstacles to new companies deploying new services had to be removed to achieve my goals. As I pushed this agenda, three leaders on the other side framed my concerns and made my life far more interesting.

Jack Valenti, a close aide to President Lyndon Johnson, was for thirty-eight years the president of the Motion Picture Association of America (MPAA). Jack, now deceased, would want me to add that he had been a decorated fighter pilot in World War II. I am glad he was on our side in the war.

Bob Bergland had served in Congress through much of the 1970s and then became Secretary of Agriculture in President Jimmy Carter's Administration. He was a lobbyist with an impressive government pedigree.

Ken Duberstein was President Reagan's last Chief of Staff, ran his own lobbying firm, and still had White House dining room privileges. He was the quintessential insider, whose business was built around advancing the interests of what economists call *rent seekers*. Duberstein remains an active part of the K Street crowd.

Each of these insiders was aggressive, a skilled advocate and had a network of important connections, especially in Congress. They worked to help their clients gain new benefits and, of course, preserve the status quo. They were very good at casting their client interests as the public's interest. These Washington impresarios might well have had a career writing docudramas with a predictable mix of fact and fiction.

## Valenti

In 1990, acting on a petition from the Fox Broadcast Network, I opened a "rulemaking" process (FCC lingo for changing the law) to determine whether there was a continuing need to preclude the broadcast networks (ABC, CBS, Fox and NBC) from owning an interest in TV programs aired in prime time—7:00 to 11:00 PM on the East Coast. I will spare you the details, but you should know that Hollywood, by virtue of the preclusion, had a lock on the primetime production business.

Jack Valenti went ballistic over my action. Even though the petition to open up primetime television to broadcast network production had been filed by one of his constituent companies, Fox, which owned 20th Century Fox movie studios, he vowed to do everything he could to defeat any change in the existing rules.

Well, you can imagine the transformative nature of this exercise in regulatory rulemaking. Commissioners, who were more accustomed to listening to some phone company executive drone on about arcane regulations, were suddenly being flattered by those who graced the big screen. Movie stars and directors were flown in and dutifully went from commissioner's office to commissioner's office. And Valenti, ever the masterful conductor, made sure each commissioner was invited to attend the Academy Awards Ceremony, as VIPs. I was not invited.

The FCC in a three-to-two vote opted for the Valenti position—the status quo. I wrote the dissenting opinion that later was embraced by the courts in overturning the FCC's majority. My dissent did not help my relations with my colleagues. Nor, by the way, do I cite this as a badge of honor. As one of my colleagues quipped, "This is a fight between the very rich and the very wealthy." You enter these kinds of fights at considerable peril.

I remember vividly one meeting with Valenti, during which he recounted the popularity of the movie nights he hosted. Valenti entertained, in the MPPA's private dining room and theater, premiere nights for key members of both Congress and the Executive Branch. My wife and I attended several.

He told me that recently, after sending out invitations for a movie night, he got a call from a member of Congress who told him the movie date was the same as the White House barbeque for members of Congress. Valenti said he would change the date. The congressman said, "Don't do that, I would rather come to your party." Valenti was a masterful politician and lobbyist and he didn't let you forget it.

# Bergland

Having watched the majority on the FCC delegate the decision over primetime television to Hollywood, I was not surprised at Senator Fritz Hollings' (D-South Carolina) delegation of authority to Secretary Bob Bergland, an esteemed member of what I had begun to consider the House of Lords of the US.

Beginning in 1990, I worked with the FCC's engineering bureau to identify a block of radio spectrum that could be used for the emerging digital mobile phone applications called PCS, or personal communications services. To say that the success of this initiative was transformative would be an understatement. Today's robust and diversified market for mobile devices and services began, in part, with it.

But along the way, I ran into Bob Bergland, then head of the National Rural Electric Cooperative Association (REA). He had served in the Carter Administration as Secretary of Agriculture. Secretary Bergland had an ally who both chaired the Senate Commerce Committee and the Senate Appropriations Subcommittee; that subcommittee had authority over the FCC's annual appropriation. Bergland's ally: Senator Hollings.

Significant FCC initiatives need to land softly on the desks of key senators. Hollings was the ultimate key senator, and his appropriation's pen was like a heat seeking missile. Committee chairmen do not like to be surprised.

I took key persons from the FCC engineering staff with me to Hollings' office to make a presentation to the senator on how we could free up spectrum for important new services by moving a few microwave users to a different spectrum corridor. I knew that if I went by myself, Hollings would do all the talking. On this occasion Hollings listened for most of ten minutes. There were no monologue prompts in the spectrum mapping presentation. A small victory.

When I arrived at the senator's office, I found Secretary Bergland sitting alongside him. We presented the senator our plan and emphasized the great potential of the new services and the added competition to the incumbent providers. We also indicated our intent to cover any out-of-pocket costs microwave users might incur in their move. Our plan required repositioning a handful of microwave services to a different spectrum position.

Hollings was unmoved. He turned to me and in his deep Southern drawl said, "Mr. Chairman, you are talking logic. I am talking politics. You make Secretary Bergland happy and I will be happy." His body language left no doubt about his intention.

My staff then spent the next month in a futile negotiation with Bergland, while I built a countervailing force on the other side of Capitol Hill. Fortunately, I was able to persuade an equally powerful and insistent Commerce Committee Chairman

John Dingell on the House side. Dingell ended up supporting the initiative, checking the power of Hollings. The FCC initiative was successfully concluded.

## Duberstein

I didn't fare too well with my third adversary, Ken Duberstein, and to a degree he didn't fare well with me. Duberstein represented the media giant Time Warner and used his White House connections to sway the same commissioners who supported Valenti. He had not appreciated my support for a change in the Financial Interest and Syndication Rule that protected Hollywood. Time Warner owned Warner Brothers, one of Hollywood's major movie studios.

At the beginning of an inquiry I initiated into the price and service implications of cable TV service being monopolized, Duberstein asked me to have lunch with him in the White House dining room. I accepted.

A few days before the lunch, a short article appeared in *US News and World Report* suggesting I was out of favor at the White House because of regulatory moves aimed at cable TV. Duberstein, citing the article, indicated that I should move on and that he could get me a job in the White House rallying support for President Bush's Desert Storm initiative, thus making a resignation more palatable. I told him I was happy at the FCC and, as he knew, had a fixed term.

Duberstein then proceeded to use his connections to make sure the swing vote on the five-member commission voted his way. Commissioner Andrew Barrett was invited to a state dinner at the White House and subsequently sided with Time Warner on cable regulation issues.

As Duberstein's clout over FCC Commissioners increased, I decided to drop any cable regulatory effort and turn to Congress. I testified before a House committee in favor of a bill to preclude cities from allowing monopoly cable franchises; competition was needed. Neither he, nor his White House friends, who purported to speak for the president, were happy with my testimony. There was no call from the president, however. White House staffers endlessly inflate their point of view by saying they speak for the president.

These and other experiences convinced me that the A-team was frequently deployed along K Street. Lobbying firms and trade associations recruited very talented and well-connected former government officials and paid them a lot of money to gain or preserve favors. Crony capitalism. I remember one colorful exchange with a constituent of Senator Hollings.

I had gone fishing with a charter boat captain out of Charleston, South Carolina. On the way to the fishing grounds, we talked about the local economy. With the Cold War over, I suggested that Charleston, a hub of military spending, would suffer. He doubted my assessment and assured me that "Old Strom and Fritz were good at getting and keeping." Strom was Strom Thurmond, South Carolina's senior senator. I spent seven years in Washington—their combined US Senate tenure was eighty-six years.

• • •

My stories are over twenty years old. And while communications issues are important, they pale in significance to the enormous deficit, annual debt, and related underfunded entitlements we face today. The cleavages between hope and reality have worsened, regardless of which political party commands a numerical majority in the Congress or occupies the White House. Actually, the most disciplined stretch of financial management occurred when Bill Clinton, a Democrat, was President and Newt Gingrich, a Republican, was Speaker of the House.

In my experience, political leadership is often secondary to cultural leadership. Washington culture leads, political leaders follow. As political leaders demonstrate their subservience to the Capitol's self-serving forces, the public loses confidence. Has it also lost hope?

We, of course, are also citizens. In January 1961, John F. Kennedy was sworn in as president. In his inaugural address he famously challenged Americans: "And so, my fellow Americans: ask not what your country can do for you—ask what you can do for your country." Americans literally gushed—the Peace Corps with its call to sacrifice became symbolic.

Yet today we fight wars in which only a few sacrifice, while most politicians specialize in pandering to special interest groups. Governments expand, debt grows and when the elected finally leave office, they don't step down but step up, at least economically, to join legions of their peers who cash in by promoting or defending some government benefit.

This unfortunate state of affairs is deeply ironic. We are mostly free to choose those who lead our public institutions, yet we disapprove of those we have chosen. And for the most part, we are free to choose the businesses from which we buy things. Too frequently we seem not to like the results of our choices. We seem caught in an undertow—free but unfree.

The undertow, most discouragingly, seems just as strong in the leader class. Many leaders get caught up in cultural forces that pull them away from community interests toward strictly private ones. And this is not just true in what we think of as the public realm. I was raised to believe that those who are fortunate enough to lead businesses also have responsibilities to their employees and community. Leadership failure is intensely discouraging and debilitating.

Meanwhile, the institution supposed to help check folly is equally disregarded. When much of the news media align its news coverage with its political leanings, only the convinced continue to pay attention and reflect confidence in them. And as noted earlier, if you watch the commercials festooning the cable news shows, it is clear that this is a very old audience. The nation needs objective curiosity across all age groups and resolve in both reporting and reading or listening.

As any successful jazz musician will explain, when earlier compositions are played, improvisation at its best honors the musical theme. My friend, Monty Alexander, a gifted jazz pianist, calls the other kind of improvisation, free jazz, "cats playing for cats." Much of what goes on in Washington today is "cats playing for cats."

Recently, Jack Danforth lost a former aide and friend, Missouri State Auditor Tom Schweich, to a self-inflicted bullet. At the time of Schweich's death, he was running for the Republican nomination for governor in Missouri.

In Jack's heartfelt eulogy, at the memorial service, he related recent conversations with Schweich about attack ads and hurtful political gossip. Jack said that in their discussions he kept coming back to the same advice: "the objective should be always to take the high ground and never give it up."

Office holders and candidates need to be constantly searching for the high ground. And perhaps at the beginning of each "high-ground meeting," a series of questions should be asked.

Let me suggest the first question. What, those seated around the table should ask, can be done to make the US government work better? Republicans will, of course, start from a conservative perspective and Democrats with the opposite. But if government is paralyzed by division caused by hard-edged polarization, everybody loses. Standing on principle is not wrong, but paralyzing government is not right.

In a democracy, we assume that officeholders that do not measure up will be removed. If only that were so. The problem today is that most congressional districts have been gerrymandered, and the cost of taking on an incumbent is measured in millions of dollars.

In 2006, a sixty-six-year-old Sudanese billionaire named Mohammed Ibrahim, who had made his fortune in telecommunications, stated, "It's my conviction that Africa doesn't need help, doesn't need aid." He went on to say that the problem is "governance—the way Africans govern themselves. Without good governance, there's no way forward."

Ibrahim's foundation started a program in 2006 to award cash prizes to leaders who leave office with relatively corruption-free records. It offers $5 million over ten years and then $200,000 a year for the rest of the leader's life. Here is how the foundation describes its initiative:

"One of the founding initiatives of the Foundation, the Ibrahim Prize, celebrates excellence in African leadership. It is awarded to a former Executive Head of State or Government by an independent Prize Committee composed of eminent figures, including two Nobel Laureates."

Since its inception, the prize has been awarded four times. One of the recipients was Nelson Mandela. In 2009, 2012 and 2013 the prize was not awarded.

We need a variation on this initiative in the US. While criteria for such an award are well beyond the scope of this book,

I would target Congress, where members often organize their voting around their monetary interests and then cash in when they leave office. Let me suggest several criteria.

If a member of Congress accepts more than a certain percentage of his/her campaign funds from interests over which they have specific congressional power, they would be disqualified. No prize. If they vote for an infrastructure project to be named for a sitting or former member of Congress, they should be disqualified. No prize. Finally, to be eligible, the member must not stay in Washington, but return to his/her home district. This last criterion shouldn't be unpalatable, since members constantly tell their constituents how much they hate living in Washington.

# CATEGORICAL FAILURE

*Effective leadership is not about making speeches or being liked; leadership is defined by results, not attributes.*

**Peter Drucker, management consultant**

Steven Covey, the author of *The Habits of Highly Effective People* encouraged people, as *The Economist* reported in July of 2012, "to divide their tasks into four categories: urgent and important; non-urgent and important; urgent and unimportant; non-urgent and unimportant."

If we assess government using the Covey method, we would find its focus especially weak in the second most important category, "non-urgent and important." Indeed, at any given point, the "urgent and important" category is filled with the failure to address what was important but non-urgent. This failure underscores the debilitation of government in the US today.

Case in point: when I began practicing law in 1964, the national debt was $312 million and 45 percent of annual gross domestic product (GDP). By the turn of the century, 2000, it had grown to $5.7 trillion and 55 percent of GDP. At the end of 2014, it was $18 trillion and 101 percent of GDP, according to the US Bureau of Economic Analysis.

It is an article of faith that crisis brings out our nation's best. Certainly after September 11, 2001, we responded quickly, although not altogether effectively. Often acting urgently compromises effectiveness.

Financial urgency, however, is more complex than responding to an enemy attack. The Great Recession, which erased enormous amounts of wealth and millions of jobs, is instructive. It took years of profligacy, often disguising home ownership as a public benefit, to wreck the nation. And since leadership failed to seriously engage with the public on the underlying issue of unsustainable debt artificially pumping up asset values, the resulting disaster came as a surprise to all but a few prescient investors noted in the Michael Lewis book and the movie *The Big Short*. I should add that only a small percentage of the public follows with any regularity Washington's legerdemain. Wonder what other surprises are lurking?

• • •

In 1986, when I began work at the Commerce Department and then in 1989 when I went across town to the FCC, good fortune was my ally. Success, more often than not, is born out of favorable circumstances. Few succeed when the wind is in their face.

By 1986, my first year in Washington, computer technology had become a promising and potentially disruptive force. We were in the early days of its impact on telecommunications, consumer electronics, and mass media.

The US had, in the post-World War II period, led the world in communications technology and services, but its leadership had become stale. Monopolization was part of the problem. AT&T was predominant, and Japan had outhustled the US consumer electronics industry. In general, telecommunication companies, preserving their government-assured advantages, had become more adept in Washington than in the marketplace. Because of the government's regulatory footprint, it needed to help lead the digital revolution, or at the very least get out of the way. While ultimately the digital revolution was not to be stopped, if it was to be encouraged, the government had to allocate new channels, facilitate new protocols, and clear out the rules that allowed a handful of companies to monopolize the most important communications businesses. Yet none of these issues required urgent attention. They were important—but not urgent. Fortunately, when I arrived at the FCC, there were few truly urgent issues facing the Commission, which certainly helped me to turn to the most important ones.

Yet it is difficult to confront important issues that are not urgent. Embedded interests specialize in protecting themselves. One faces, to understate the problem, institutional resistance. Elected politicians war over what to do, collect checks from the interested parties, and engage in dynamic inaction; bureaucrats are complicit, as they generally favor the status quo. The FCC had divisions and bureaus and sections and the jobs that went with them, all organized around rapidly obsolescing technology. Government bureaucracies are intensely conservative—reform is often perceived to be the enemy. In commercial markets, however, America enjoys an enormous advantage, because in most countries, governments are much more intrusive in business affairs.

As the misalignment of government policies and realities have become more insistent, America's leaders have been increasingly confronted with important issues that seethe but don't erupt: underfunded entitlement programs, chaotic tax laws and regulations, and deferred maintenance of public infrastructure, to name a few. Each has been accorded kick-the-can-down-the-road treatment as one or another sensation captures the few minutes we are prepared to spend on a public issue. We, the public, are distractible as the constant swing of what is most important in the public polls vacillates.

As I have experienced government work on the inside, and as I have observed it from the outside, it is a case study in negligence. Indeed, increasingly critics claim criminal negligence as politicians accept big checks from special interests for their campaigns. Bribery is the charge.

In 2015, the nation now faces a bewildering array of both

urgent and important issues. Yet we are an advanced nation that has advanced to the point where true progress is maddeningly difficult. I am reminded of a friend's quip that "working in New York City adds points to your IQ." I think the opposite is true in Washington.

• • •

I was in New York on September 11, 2001. I was not downtown where the attack on the World Trade Centers occurred, but watched the dense smoke from midtown. Later in the day, I watched as subway, train and bus commuters were turned into pedestrians. Shock, anger and grief competed in defining the facial expressions of all New Yorkers, but in particular those who trudged north on foot toward their homes in upper Manhattan or the suburbs. Most major arteries in and out of Manhattan were closed.

I can recall with pride leaders of both parties coming together in both patriotic song and action. I can remember a church service in Manhattan led by a pastor, rabbi and imam. People thought and acted big; leaders responded.

Today political rhetoric drives us apart. The two parties engage in endless fighting over how to divide up the revenue and debt pool. We lack the leadership to rally America around political and economic solutions. As the fall of 2015 closes, Donald Trump is the latest "man on a white horse" whose rhetoric is filled with anger instead of insight. Some believe he is poised to head the party of Lincoln, Theodore Roosevelt, Eisenhower and Reagan.

Every problem, or so it seems, is presented as a part of a demographic war. We are divided by clever politicians and their operatives into classes and sub-classes who are fighting a zero-sum game.

Computers, of course, are increasingly used to convert voters into data inventory organized by race, geography, education, income, creed, voting patterns, and psychographics. And then the operatives—the political version of *Mad* Men—take over. They dramatize real differences while manufacturing others.

Opponents are either too religious or insufficiently so. Conservatives are far right and liberals far left. Opposition research goes back to a candidate's college years or probes family members. And since virtually all politicians at the federal level are rich, various struggle narratives are developed to show empathy or antipathy. And on and on.

Words without a sharp edge are redefined to have one. Principled public figures who are also realists are called moderates. In the Republican Party, moderates are said to be establishment figures, and in certain parts of the party, being a moderate is only slightly better than being a Bolshevik.

In the Democratic Party, the realistic engage insufficiently in identity politics. Rarely does anybody who strives to appeal to the Democrat base criticize the far left, and when they do it is said to be a "Sister Souljah moment." Sister Souljah, in a media interview, suggested that blacks who want to kill should kill whites—not other blacks. Then-candidate Bill Clinton denounced such a sentiment. If coming out against killing is an act of courage, then courage is without meaning.

I admit that there was a time, many decades ago, when I seriously thought about running for Congress. Today I cannot imagine a less attractive ambition. And to me that is the overarching problem—not my not running, but the abandonment of the two political parties by leaders who have been hijacked by realism.

Politics, the often emotional ways and means of governance, has been disfigured by people who assert that they are going to elevate public discourse and provide government solutions, and then spend all their time demonizing the other party or candidate. The public is not fooled. Gallup and other research organizations capture the disgust.

What is missing is a compelling narrative that might renew one of the most important acts of citizenship—political involvement.

The alignment of voters with political parties has declined precipitously. I can understand why a thoughtful person would regard becoming an independent as a worthy move. But in a nation where the laws are heavily tilted in favor of the two predominant political parties, abandonment of party politics risks an abandonment of active citizenship.

As voters leave one or the other party, the ideologues and self-interested take over; they become the base. If you belong to a public employee union, the odds are overwhelming that you are a Democrat and urge your leaders to fight for all your benefits. If you are a Republican, then even a whiff of a tax increase causes the Club for Growth to damn the candidate. As a practical matter, this forecloses tax reform and results in wars being funded by debt. Had George W. Bush called for a tax increase to fund the wars in Afghanistan and Iraq, Grover Norquist, Washington's principal anti-tax political operative, would have attacked.

If the body politic was a computer, the advice would be to reboot. Unfortunately, a political reboot won't happen without talented leaders and compelling narratives. And when you hear the base of either party attack a candidate as a heretic, that is somebody to whom you should pay close attention. When the momentum is dysfunctional, we need some heretics.

Today's politicians are mostly sound-bite artists. They are consumed by what they perceive to be the imperatives of the next election. And of course, the first step is to curry favor with those who finance the campaigns or round up the votes. The financier's interests are mostly narrow self-interests. Truly patriotic money is often on the sidelines, sickened by the options.

The candidates who choose the Republican side are more familiar to me. All Republican candidates wrap themselves in the Reagan flag and vow to vote or act as he would. Really. Regardless of what one thinks about Reagan's policies, they were organized by a vision of America that was uniquely personal and principled.

And what about Reagan's pragmatism, or what I prefer to call realism? Reagan raised taxes. He made deals with the Democratic Speaker of the House, Tip O'Neill. He supported the Brady bill, which regulated the sale of firearms. He was a very effective leader, in part, because his oft and well-stated vision caused him to get the better end of most bargains, and his voter chemistry was excellent.

But today on both wings of the spectrum, there is little discernable thinking. There are, of course, exceptions, but most politicians seem to have stored their sound bites in their memory and then use their processing power to recall rhetorical fragments based on associated prompts. Most are in default mode. America can no longer flourish in default mode.

This state of affairs results in gotcha politics. Candidates are subjected to intense scrutiny and their few spontaneous moments and their lifestyle are given enormous weight, too much in my view. Mitt Romney might have made a good president, but he couldn't overcome the accoutrements of serious wealth paired with unartful, and perhaps revealing, comments about 47 percent of Americans receiving some sort of a government check.

As I finish this book, the ego-driven bombastic Donald Trump's standings in the polls tells us all we need to know about our nation's disrepair.

Pope Francis, in a November, 2014 address to the European Parliament, noted "The great ideas that once inspired Europe seem to have lost their attraction, only to be replaced by the bureaucratic technicalities of its institutions." America is not far behind.

Too many candidates and their flaks luxuriate in adding this or that new program, proclaiming that America will now produce more jobs, more equality, more fairness or whatever.

The War on Poverty, launched in the 1960s, was going to end poverty. Need I say more?

On the right, any increase in marginal tax rates is regarded as heretical. So, as noted, the Afghanistan and Iraq wars, beginning as they did at a moment of great unity and patriotism, were nonetheless funded with debt.

Is it possible to talk in terms of values and their essential role in optimizing human potential?

In a March 15, 2015 article in *The Atlantic*, titled "Choose Your Own Enlightenment," Dominic Green observed,

> *If we outsource the intellectual labor of decision-making to the upper crust, or surrender to the bread and circuses of digital entertainment, we cannot complain about the results. Long ago, before the Enlightenment, people cowered before governments and speech laws. The Enlightenment offered an alternative, but it is one that must continually be affirmed: by public actions, by intellectual engagement, and by voting. We must make our own Enlightenment, or be chosen by someone Else's.*

• • •

When I left my hometown of Sikeston, my parents had made sure I was not an innocent. They also made sure their values had been imparted—whether they took or not.

I then spent seven years learning about the world from a variety of professors and books. But perhaps the most telling instruction was early in law school, when a professor gesturing toward the immense library of law books said, "When you leave you won't know a percent of what is in those books, but you will know what you don't know and how to find out what you need to know."

Only when the governed are actively curious and involved will governors act responsibly. The election ballot can be assured and its secrecy protected, but an incurious electorate informed principally by interest group advocates and political commercials will not protect our exceptional country. Exceptionalism does not come with a guarantee.

Is it possible to envision a nation of effectual governance at each level, and thoughtful candidates and office holders who understand that Washington, America's central government, no longer works well? Ironically, those who want a central government to do more and more are asking for a central government that does less and less well, while piling up debt that is passed on to the next generation. Or, perhaps we could join Argentina and ask that our financial promises be forgiven or at least discounted.

# THE AXIS

*If you worship money and things, if they are where you tap real meaning in life, then you will never have enough, never feel you have enough... Worship power, you will end up feeling weak and afraid, and you will need ever more power over others to numb you to your own fear.*

David Foster Wallace, author and professor

I left Washington for New York because I like adventures. In the world of business—perhaps in the world itself—New York has an almost incandescent quality. How could I turn down the opportunity?

My departure from the FCC was somewhat abrupt. I had hoped to stay through the summer of 1993, when my term expired. I could have, but when Bill Clinton defeated President Bush, I quickly changed my mind. Simply stated, when the White House changes hands, the appointees of the soon-to-be-replaced president should clean out their offices. Also, the months between the election and President Clinton's inauguration were instructive on the misery of the lame duck. While power has its downsides, its absence is miserable. In Washington, the power of ideas is secondary to one's future power, and I had none.

Of course, I did get numerous offers to stay in Washington as an *advocate*—generic for Washington attorney or lobbyist. I was momentarily a minor celebrity and well connected. I had gone from disconnected to *connected* in seven years. And in Washington there is a self-protective culture. If you have been a chairman or a secretary or an ambassador or a member of Congress, you are accorded a level of deference for life, whether it is deserved or not. There is, as earlier noted, an informal House of Lords—the British, having a formal one, are more transparent. But I decided to leave the "Lords" and the *Mr. Chairman* honorific and go to the city of commercial power. My mind was focused briefly, however, on the Lords as I considered several Washington offers. There is an almost seamless opportunity to go from political to commercial power.

One of America's problems is its House of Lords. Tip O'Neill, a former Speaker, once quipped that "all politics is local." True to a point. Also true to a point is that much of politics is relational. Washington is awash in current officeholders helping former ones and expecting the same treatment when they are ready to retire and cash in. At one level this is expected and understandable; but the cumulative effect is insidious and precludes any real priority setting. Every program and expenditure and deduction and credit has a well-heeled constituency.

In Washington, the House of Lords was wealth's vehicle. I was offered approximately $500,000 more than I was being paid by the FCC to change positions—from power holder to power influencer.

Several years after arriving in New York, a dinner party that included David Rubenstein, the founder and CEO of The Carlyle Group, captured the choice I faced in my departure year. I was seated next to Rubenstein and we were talking about Bill Kennard, a former FCC Chairman, who had recently joined The Carlyle Group.

The Carlyle Group, as Wikipedia summarizes it, is "a global asset management firm, specializing in private equity, based in Washington, D.C." It operates in four business areas:

corporate private equity, real assets, global market strategies, and investment solutions." David has built a very successful company and is a noted philanthropist. *Forbes* estimates his wealth at $2.9 billion; it would be much higher if he were not so generous.

Rubenstein asked me questions about Kennard and said he had hopes Kennard would become a business partner. I asked him about the high-profile former government leaders who were associated with his company. They included former President George H. W. Bush and his Secretary of State, Jim Baker. Rubenstein said they were expected to open doors, not make business decisions. He hoped Kennard could do the latter, not just the former.

I had a lot of door-opening offers; but only two would let me return to business. The offer I took was to join The Hearst Corporation in New York City to start a new group of digital businesses. At the time, Hearst and every other media company were wholly analog (modulation of sine waves) in their media design, production and distribution. All analog media was one-way unless the consumer wanted to use the Post Office or an 800 number. Yet we were on the cusp of unlimited channels and interactivity. I was on the cusp of a real adventure.

As I found, no part of the wealth engine worked better or earlier in life than Wall Street, New York's leading business sector. If a company could show Wall Street non-stop earnings growth, its executives would get rich and in the process those who handled their equity and debt offerings and acquisition and merger transactions would be similarly rewarded.

The New York wealth engine had consequences for the Sikes family. When Marty and I moved, we had to borrow money to buy our apartment. Never had we spent more money for less room. Later we learned that Fifth Avenue apartments were bought with bonus checks by Wall Street twentysomethings and thirtysomethings.

Moving to New York gives you a choice; every lifestyle exists in the city.

The apartment we occupied was on the Upper East Side, where *Worth Magazine* at the outset of the 21st century calculated the cost of annual living for a fictional family of four living the good life. They concluded the annual cost would be $497,416, including staff, exclusive schools, rent on a second home in the Hamptons and the like. That is $497,416 in after-tax dollars, requiring almost $1 million in taxable income.

Thankfully, my family's appetites were not on that list. Of course a lot of those dollars, for many of the privileged, are family trust dollars.

According to the Commerce Department's Bureau of Economic Analysis in a 2012 report, Manhattan had a median family income of $75,629 in 2011. To get to the bottom of the New York State county income list you just need to travel several dozen blocks to arrive in Bronx County with a median family income of $38,431.

In 1993, my emotions and sensibilities were in motion. I felt pulled home, but knew that my seven years in the middle of a technological revolution made my return difficult, even though I would from time to time wish for the softer edges of the Midwest.

When I started a radio company in Missouri 16 years earlier, my objective had been to acquire a group of small-market AM and FM radio stations. In New York, I was surrounded by people who thought only at the big city and network levels.

New York broadcasters wanted to own as many stations as the law would allow, and this ambition insisted on a national footprint. I realized how modest my ambitions had been. Power in New York required counting a lot of chips.

New York measures you every single day. No place in the world is so unrelenting. In Washington you can hide—there are plenty of good jobs where dynamic inaction will suffice; the government doesn't know how to measure. Smarts, a quick tongue and the ability to create and nurture a network of patrons will a career make.

In the Midwest, where I started my career, they measure differently. Modest successes by New York standards are successes. In New York, modest successes don't play on Broadway or Wall Street. And neither asks how you got there. If the talent or money measure up, how you got there, if outrageous enough, is another bestseller.

New York, as well, seems to exert a mogul force. Some are drawn to the conclusion that an assemblage of assets that will earn one true mogul status is the only acceptable ultimate ambition.

Now don't get me wrong: ambition is good. It goes with striving; its absence stultifies. Ambition and success in the material world are symbiotic. Ambition, however, comes with its dark side. Too many transform the lower-case gods to which their ambition attaches into upper case ones.

Washington is a mix of idealism and personal ambition, at least at the beginning; New York's North Star, however, is personal ambition from beginning to end.

A generation or two later, most children of immigrants are pleased at the personal or family ambition of their ancestors. And the accompanying sacrifice made by the first generation is often a poignant story. A New York-magnitude ambition often has a good ending—but only, if, as the personal ambition evolves, it is softened with at least a modicum of humility.

Washington ambition by comparison, disengaged from at least lingering idealism and humility, is corrosive, and our nation's publicity machine exerts a strong pull to the purely personal. Effectual power results from not caring who gets credit; the most ambitious Washington politicians, however, are addicted to their images on the TV screen. They want credit and their publicists orchestrate the news so it lasts for more than one news cycle.

New York pushes and pushes everybody who signs up to make more and more money. Washington then passes laws aimed at both real and imaginary abuses attributed to the concentration of market power. And at times, Washington and New York seem to collaborate on excess. The axis is clear.

We are still living in the backlash of what became known as The Great Recession; it was caused by the inexorable force of money and Washington's periodic pursuit of utopia, in this case universal home ownership and the mortgage guarantees that went with that. When Washington gets in the middle of markets, New York pays attention—Wall Street securitized the debt. Subsidized and protected markets are bubble engines—and bubbles always burst.

I began talking about leadership in the stream-based world of trout, noting the necessity of wariness and agility in escaping predators. At the level of hyper-ambition, predation is not only understood, it often becomes the goal. Variations on "survival of the fittest" is often the model of behavior.

When Darwinian leadership becomes the default template, we are all at risk of being seen as prey. Fortunately, my family's modest business and small retailers in general receive almost instantaneous feedback. Chiseling at the expense of your customers is certain to destroy a community-based retail business. Capitalism's most important corrective is organic to the customer relationship.

Unfortunately, in many media and financial products (those I know best), that is not the case. Financial products, notwithstanding their pages of small print, are wrapped up in simple advertising narratives of consumer bliss.

Media frequently appeal to the lowest common denominator and when their coarseness is criticized, the companies wrap themselves in the flag of free speech, as if to coarsen society were somehow a patriotic act.

Such entertainment, shaped by words, music and images don't come with warranties. When the lowest common denominator template becomes dominant, society becomes prey.

I enjoy movies, both old and new; they can be especially magnetic and some even force us to confront our life's direction.

Recently, my wife and I were watching a 1963 movie, Hud, starring Paul Newman, Patricia O'Neal and Melvyn Douglas. The setting: a cattle ranch in Texas that was just hanging on when it was hit by an outbreak of hoof-and-mouth disease.

The movie pitted a hard drinking, unprincipled son, Hud (played by Paul Newman) against his father, Homer (played by Melvyn Douglas), the patriarch owner of the ranch and a moralist at heart. The two men often argued in front of an impressionable and idealistic young man, Lon (played by Brandon de Wilde) who was grandson to Homer and nephew to Hud.

In one memorable scene, Homer said to Lon after a furious argument with Hud, "Little by little the look of the country changes because of the men we admire....You're just going to have to make up your own mind one day about what's right and wrong." And so it is, although today we would say "the men and women we admire."

# FREE MARKETS

*Half the harm that is done in this world is due to people who want to feel important. They don't mean to do harm; but the harm does not interest them. Or they do not see it, or they justify it because they are absorbed in the endless struggle to think well of themselves.*

**T.S. Eliot, *The Waste Land***

*Management is doing things right; leadership is doing the right things.*

**Peter Drucker, management consultant, educator and author**

The visuals were just as important as the words. My introduction to business remains vivid and timeless.

In those early years, I cleaned up and then clerked in my grandparents' hardware store. It followed the small-town pattern of carrying way more than hardware, and was on Front Street in Sikeston, Missouri; population 12,000.

My grandmother was more drawn to business, Granddad to farming. "Gram" was almost always at the store.

The store was boxy and wouldn't have inspired Norman Foster's architectural imagination. Its most distinctive characteristic was a large glass front. My grandparents, Leah and Alfred Sikes and then later their two sons, John and Kendall (my father), were often on the first floor helping customers. In the jargon of today, their business was transparent to their customers.

There was also an unusual gathering spot in the store. Most of the customers built and fixed things and carried pocketknives. There was a horseshoe counter around the stairs that led to the store's basement and on the counter were sharpening stones. Men would pause to sharpen their knives and exchange the latest stories and opinions—social media, circa the 1940s and '50s. There is a conceit that multi-tasking is somehow the invention of the Computer Age. Amusing.

Each day began at 7:30 and ended at 5:30. Their customers didn't need to navigate a bureaucracy or call an 800 number to offer their opinion or criticism about merchandise or service. The owners were available and approachable. Business success turned on their customers' satisfaction and, as my Dad would often say, "being a part of the community."

Two generations after clerking in the family business, I arrived in New York City to create a new business, in a new technology, on a big stage. As Dad noted at the time, "Son, you are in tall cotton."

Tall cotton means a rich harvest. But having picked cotton, I knew that walking on your knees through the rows of cotton plants obstructs vision. You could see the next plant, but little else. In some ways, global business is not much different.

As I learned in New York City and other citadels of commerce, customer relationships are represented by a stream of data. Our demographic profile, daily buying patterns, viewing habits and social media engagement comprise our profile. Profit-center executives track these profiles and translate them into supply and demand detail and findings.

While a cotton picker could not see much beyond the next cotton plant, executives choose not to see much beyond their data sheets. I worry less about the loss of privacy—today's primary focus—than about the loss of humanity. What happens when a culture is abstracted by data by those who feel no cultural responsibility? There are no avatars with human-like profiles, and interactions as marketers parse the data. Community and its dynamic are irrelevant.

The CEO routine in New York is to walk out the door of an apartment building or a home in the suburbs and into a company car with a driver. Often, overnight files of new customer sales data await the CEO as he travels to the office building, gets on an elevator and rides to, let's say, the 46nd floor.

In the media industry, the focus on the way to work is often the overnight numbers indicating how many eyeballs were watching your shows or playing your games. I'm not making that up: media people distill viewers into *eyeballs* as they discuss viewing data. Abstracting data masks the messy world in which we live.

The 46nd Floor C Suite, which houses a company's executive leadership, is an important symbol. Its occupants have arrived. Their business acumen rewards them with luxurious offices, spacious boardrooms and elegant private dining. This is most often on top of seven-figure or eight-figure salaries plus stock or option grants. In 2013, CEO pay for the top 200 companies averaged $20.7 million consisting of $6.8 million in cash and the rest in stocks and options, according to a June 2014 article by Robert J. Samuelson in *The Washington Post*.

Granddad had an office as well. When he left the merchandise floor, he retreated to a small space adjacent to the stock room, where inventory was stored.

Dad's dining room was one of several booths in a Walgreens, about a block from the store. Generally around 9 a.m., you could find him and a rotating cast of friends conversing over coffee, instead of reading reams and reams of data from the various corporate outposts. In community retailing, there were no "Chateau Generals," as George Marshall called World War II generals who spent their time at headquarters.

Okay, I know, sentimentalism is often blind. The world of my grandparents had its robber barons, and retailing is different than making and distributing things. But, and this is the central point, fewer and fewer of the people who command banking or media or manufacturing or service industries have any connection to the actual customer. Much of what was sold at Sikes Hardware is now sold by Wal-Mart, Home Depot and Costco; all mammoth, big-box stores. The customer's life is largely an abstraction, a data profile, continuously updated by optical scanners and online purchasing. There is nothing wrong with following supply and demand data, unless nothing else is followed.

How many retail bankers who initiated zero down-payment home loans knew the newly minted debtors? And of course none of the investment bankers who securitized the loans knew them. Their obtuseness, along with government guarantees, helped tank the economy and the well-being of millions who saw the value of their most important asset dramatically reduced. Home values in all but the most prosperous zip codes fell precipitously.

The customer's family is another piece of data summarized by demographers, surveyors, and untold numbers of commercial sociologists. When that data also reveals the social pathologies of a society shaped by consumerism, it is all too inviting to retreat to the 46th floor and read trade journals that highlight the wonders of your industry.

And the dreams of abundance that waft through the 46th-floor imaginations tend to define our age. When Humphrey Bogart in *Key Largo* asks mob boss Edward G. Robinson what Robinson wants, Robinson quips, "I just want more." Too often today we just want more, and damn the consequences.

Dennis Kozlowski, the former CEO of Tyco who in 2005 was convicted of looting his company in the form of illegal bonuses, was recently paroled. Kozlowski and a colleague admitted to stealing $150 million. At a parole hearing, Kozlowski said, "I fell into what I can best describe as a CEO bubble, and I rationalized that I was more valuable than I was."

There were no bubbles where I grew up and, as a radio broadcaster, I finally rebelled when Tipper Gore highlighted the lyrics of hard rock music. I appreciated the chance to read the lyrics in an industry publication, *Radio and Records*, as they were hard for my forty-year-old ears to make out and deemed inappropriate for a family newspaper. Too bad; parents need to know the content of their children's music.

I told my program director at a station I owned in the Cape Girardeau, Missouri market (KJAQ) to remove certain songs from the play list. He was not happy.

If I had run a network of big city radio stations, somebody in the recording industry might have paid some attention. But reflecting on my time at the FCC, there was never a moment when a radio network executive or recording executive criticized the content of song lyrics. They simply recorded and played the hits and reviewed the overnight listening data.

• • •

It is not possible to be a consumer without marveling at the bounty of free market capitalism. And let me add, to be awestruck by the inventiveness and energy of innovators. It is also not possible for me to relegate New York City to a money machine. Its neighborhoods, its ethnicity, its arts, its dynamism were summed up by a friend who called it "the great indoors." I should add that its interior spaces enjoy bold relief as Central Park invites everybody outside.

So my distaste for media capitalism, unplugged, did not have a comfortable beginning. Perhaps part of my problem was that my interest and ultimate career began in an especially encouraging setting.

As a high school student I was given a chance to intern at KSIM radio station in Sikeston. I did little more than help the news director keep track of the Associated Press news ticker and put records back in the music library. I did, however, become a sort of insider, because I usefully relieved the on-air personalities from having to do monotonous work, and they were appreciative.

I remember the enjoyment of knowingly listening to Sikeston's sole source of music, news and commercials that promoted local businesses. I knew what went on behind the scenes—a fleeting moment of self-importance.

Radio broadcasting preceded the 1934 Communications Act, which made law of fact. The Act stated that broadcasters were to operate their stations in the "public interest." KSIM certainly did. So when I moved to the ownership side a generation later, I anticipated this was both a good business opportunity but also one that would give me a chance, regardless of how small, to make a positive difference in the community.

But as my broadcast career unfolded, I felt cultural pressures to operate outside what I perceived as the public interest. I was well downstream from the pop culture makers and didn't relish being their final distribution link with little discretion. I cared about the song's story.

In reality, all products, and especially media products, are parts of stories. One of my first meetings at the FCC was with an activist group that sought to limit TV productions targeting children. Program producers popularized characters (often animated characters), which were then licensed to toymakers, made into toys, quickly became must-have gifts, and generated royalty revenue. This has been a recurring complaint and the Constitution's guarantee of free speech precludes any significant government action. If the culture does not punish the exploitation of children, it will persist.

Advertisements as well need to be understood as narratives. The advertiser wants his short narrative to alter the way we look at the world occupied by his product or the way we look at ourselves. Consumers are drawn into an alternative world through artful vignettes and their repetition and then the alternative becomes real, at least for a little while.

We are now moving rapidly into a world of robotics. A world in which artificial intelligence will largely replace the human touch. Our current preoccupation with "more" will be the robots' mission. We need more poets. Most importantly, we need millennials to push back.

As I write, one of the newest health stories is about "energy drinks." In 2012, the frequency of visits to the emergency room due to adverse effects from energy drinks had doubled.

One of my aimless activities is watching a few sporting events each week. All those who watch games have been inundated with TV ads aimed at men about the various benefits of energy drinks. Better personality! Better sex! Better job interview! If only Ponce De Leon had been able to defer his search for the "fountain of youth" to the 21st Century!

And of course, if I were to go back a few years, it seemed like the entire ad inventory for televised games was being consumed by erectile dysfunction ads, with their promise of never-ending sexual bliss. Indeed, our government now includes Viagra and its lookalikes in Medicare coverage. But I digress.

This bombardment is not limited to adults. I have grandsons

who like sports and frequently watch ESPN. I suspect they see dozens of ads weekly, structured around the party narrative. All of the revelers—guys and bikini-clad gals—are drinking beer and, of course, having a great time. And then we read story after story about date rape on college campuses.

Advertising is defensible. It conveys information. It gives new companies a chance to get their message out. At the same time, it is culturally influential. And when it comes to children, the advertisers are often preying on immature minds.

Madison Avenue's Mad Men are constantly integrating consumption and cultural ideals. They specialize in contrasting our self-esteem with their ideal: mostly unreal physiques, beauty, sexual prowess, contemporary cachet and consumption in general.

Dana Jennings, a *New York Times* reporter, wrote an article headlined: "Sacked by the Media Blitz." He spent an afternoon watching an NFL game or mainly the advertisements. He came up with a new acronym: ACS, Ad Concussion Syndrome. He reported that there were well over one hundred ads "spliced into each game."

Jennings' bottom line in sport's event advertising: "male insecurity." He noted that the ad narratives used cars, trucks, beer, erectile dysfunction products, and the like as objects that will help men overcome their insecurity. But let me get back to children.

Gina Otto is the author of *Cassandra's Angel*. She left the media industry after deciding that she didn't want her life defined by the latest Diet Coke commercial.

Gina's book and school talks are aimed at helping children feel good about themselves. When she meets with young girls, she explains what happens to the youthful models that star in youth magazine and TV commercials. She confides that fashion and cosmetic and lighting experts spend hours with the models before the first image is captured.

We all know many who do not like what goes on behind the curtain yet feel they are mere subjects in a hierarchical game. Is a countervailing force possible?

Gina Otto reminds me of Candy Lightner.

# PUSHING BACK

*I'm mad as hell and I'm not going to take it anymore!*
**Howard Beale, character in the movie *Network***

On May 3$^{rd}$ in 1980, thirteen-year-old Cari Lightner was walking to a school carnival in Fair Oaks, California, when a drunk struck her from behind, killing her. The driver had three prior drunk driving convictions and was out on bail from a hit-and-run arrest two days earlier. That same year, Cari's mother, Candy Lightner, founded Mothers Against Drunk Driving (MADD).

Just four years later, MADD had grown to 330 chapters in 47 states. And since its founding, it has been instrumental in raising the legal age limit for drinking to twenty-one, lowering the illegal blood alcohol content level, and stiffening the penalties for drunk driving. By 1993, statistics revealed that alcohol-related traffic deaths had dropped to a 30-year low.

MADD not only made drunken driving laws tougher, it vividly painted a new invisible line. It transformed the mind's tripwire. The humorous drunk was increasingly seen as a weapon. His behavior became immoral. The same transformation happened with smoking, which went from sexy to filthy to borderline immoral. Smart, concerted citizen action can similarly cast discrete actions of advertisers, entertainment professionals and their corporate supporters as child predation.

Candy Lightner got mad and formed MADD. Change began at what we call the "grass roots." America is like that. Over and over people get mad and act. And if their anger is broadly shared, sometimes their actions are writ large.

• • •

Communications technology is light years beyond what existed in 1980. In 2007 Steve Jobs, then Apple's CEO, declared as he introduced the first generation iPhone, "This will change everything." He turned out to be right, to a degree. Today the smartphone with the processing power of yesterday's super-computer is ubiquitous. Social media, email networks, texting and the like facilitate rapid and inexpensive outreach. Today citizens can become leaders, organize across the boundaries that separate us, and push back.

An early intervention by my mother didn't change everything, but it certainly had an impact on my life.

As I was choosing a set of classes for my junior year in high school, Mom vetoed one choice. I had decided to take shop, a class that taught male teenagers to use tools. Mom insisted I take typing.

As I recall there was one other male in the typing class and the occupational interest of many was to become a secretary. Little did I know that this was a first step in my ultimate immersion in technology. Those who learned the secretarial skills of typing often learned coding and decoding, or what was then called shorthand. Coding, decoding and keyboarding are gateway skills in much of the technology world.

I began working with computers in the 1970s. My wife and I computerized the broadcasting business we owned. I remember well the use of VisiCalc to prepare cash flow projections and, when email communications first began, I was one of the few in my peer group with any agility on the keyboard. Thank you, Mom.

Even today I run into male executives who don't use email or, for that matter, the keyboard. They might be better with a wrench, but in today's economy it is hard to understand what you don't use.

This brings me to Mary Schmich, and ultimately to the mothers who I believe will take the lead in pushing back.

In 1997, Mary, a rather obscure columnist, wrote a column for the *International Herald Tribune* fantasizing about what she would say if she was asked to deliver a commencement address. She began her faux address:

"Wear sunscreen. If I could offer you only one tip for the future, sunscreen would be it. The long-term benefits of sunscreen have been proved by scientists; the rest of my advice has no basis more reliable than my own meandering experience."

Mary went on to counsel the graduates to floss, stretch, get plenty of calcium, sing, dance, avoid beauty magazines, and most tellingly for me, because I then lived and worked in New York City, she advised: "Live in New York City once, but leave before it makes you hard."

Mary Schmich's satirical take on commencement addresses became a national sensation because it was forwarded by an anonymous sender, in an email.

The anonymous sender typed in the subject line: "Kurt Vonnegut's commencement address at MIT." This purported Vonnegut address was then forwarded hundreds, then thousands, then tens of thousands of times. Millions read the satire and Mary Schmich's work became Kurt Vonnegut's. Since Vonnegut was a distinguished author and Schmich's work was in many ways brilliant satire, an unintended collaboration ensued.

There was a certain justice to what happened. Ms. Schmich's irreverent art deserved to be read and was praised. Better, of course, that she had been recognized as Mary Schmich.

Eighteen years later, it is much more likely that this satire could have found legs without the artful deception. As computers and related devices have become ubiquitous and networks have been facilitated by Facebook, Twitter and a variety of other social media, there are connectors of all sorts that are looking for fresh or clever insights. And there are so-called mainstream columnists like David Brooks who look for serious work by unbranded writers, and then share their names and essays.

What is certain is that the Establishment will not reform the Establishment, even though many business leaders will find a way to be close to their customers, not just their data profiles.

And the political parties and those who run for office will mostly be pulled along by their base, the intense minority, the funders and those special interests, like the National Rifle Association (NRA) and National Education Association (NEA), who represent narrow and self-interested constituencies.

Business leaders like Bill Gates have written books recently about capitalism's underbelly and encouraged a new approach. Gates called for "creative capitalism," John Mackey, the founder of Whole Foods called for "conscious capitalism," while the noted academic, Michael Porter, called for "shared-value capitalism."

These books and others are, of course, welcome. And indeed, many businessmen and women are real leaders and work to make their companies both more profitable and responsible. Capitalism works. But that is not enough. Free markets means what it says; everybody with a pulse is free to begin a business— real leaders and the pretenders.

And most people can now push back when businesses prey on the unsuspecting. Business went global some decades ago and with global scale many businesses became even more powerful and lost any real connection with their customers. Smartphones and global networks now enable activists to go global.

When I chaired the FCC, I was called on frequently by Rupert Murdoch and Barry Diller. Murdoch owned News Corporation, which owned both Fox Studios and the Fox broadcast network. Diller ran the latter. Using the FCC's pro-competition policy, they argued that the FCC should ease regulations—financial interest and syndication rules—that made it difficult for them to start a viable fourth network. My distaste for Fox's early programming made the necessary action of easing entry restrictions unpalatable.

Fox, you might recall, followed the Murdoch pattern. Murdoch had, among other things, built much of his newspaper success around tabloid journalism. And he didn't have any scruples about the content of primetime TV programming. The raunchy *Married with Children* defined his approach. I received thousands of letters at the FCC asking me to shut it down.

At the time, *Common Sense Media's* review of *Married with Children* noted:

> *Parents need to know that this show—which was purposely designed to test the boundaries of network primetime TV—mines adult themes for laughs; caution is recommended when allowing tweens and young teens to watch. References to sexual behavior (including masturbation) fly fast and furiously, there are crude references to body parts and homosexuality, and characters constantly insult and belittle each other.*

Predictably, the established big three networks (ABC, CBS, and NBC) began to imitate Fox and I had to tell the parents who wrote me, worried about its influence on their children, that a higher principle, free speech, stopped me from doing anything.

Business attitudes today need to be influenced by a variation on Larry Page's 10X theory of creative business leadership.

Page is a co-founder of Google and its current CEO. In a *Wired* magazine interview in January 2013, he said,

> *I worry that something has gone seriously wrong with the way we run companies. If you read the media coverage of our company or of the technology industry in general, it's always about the competition. The stories are written as if they are covering a sporting event. But it's hard to find actual examples of really amazing things that happened solely due to competition. How exciting is it to come to work if the best you can do is trounce some other company that does roughly the same thing? That's why most companies decay slowly over time.*

In recent years, craft beers have become a growing part of the beer industry. Recently a craft brewer, Hill Farmstead Brewery, has enjoyed critical acclaim and its owner, Shawn Hill, has been urged to expand. His response to a *New York Times* reporter, "I didn't start this brewery so I could keep growing and move it away from here; that wasn't the point. It wouldn't be fun anymore. It wouldn't have purpose or meaning."

Is growth by all means non-criminal an objective that has "purpose and meaning?" We live in a time where often creativity serves growth instead of growth coming because of creativity. What is the cultural impact when growth by virtually any means becomes the capitalist's ambition?

Pope Francis, quoting a 4th-century bishop, recently called the unfettered pursuit of money "the dung of the devil." Predictably, those who believe the only true measure of capitalistic success is shareholder return were critical. But if success has no greater meaning than return on investment (ROI), then the underlying worldview is Darwinian. When that is the worldview, then capitalism and faith in God co-exist uncomfortably.

I must, of course, quickly pull back from the existential. Simply stated, I believe businesspeople should constantly look for that sublime blend of profit seeking, cushioned by generosity and prudence. It is not always easy to find. I can recall moments in my business career when I chose profit over employee benefits, for example, believing that only the former would assure sustainability.

But we can keep in mind that a change in business practices often follows customers pushing back.

There is no reason today that concerned mothers, who made up the critical mass of those I heard from at the FCC, cannot use today's smartphones and social networks and achieve ten times what Candy Lighter did. I say this not to diminish what she did, but to point to a more complicated objective. Influencing the culture in a significant way is far more difficult than changing laws against drunk driving. Indeed the cultural machinery is in the process of transforming Cannabis sativa from dope to recreational marijuana.

And I should add that maybe the next goal of the media business should be to strive to keep or put humanity back in its products, especially those aimed at young people.

# BUBBLES

*The bottom line is no longer simply the bottom line.*

Felix Rohatyn, American investment banker

*In an obvious sense we take money too seriously today. But less obviously we do so only because we don't take money seriously enough—to understand it.*

Os Guinness, English author and social critic

My second year in New York, 1994, was on the eve of what Alan Greenspan, some years later, called a period of "irrational exuberance." Greenspan was referring to the telecommunication and dot-com bubbles. My New York job was to build a dot-com business at the Hearst Corporation.

A Hearst colleague, Gill Maurer, had an artistic bent and often used his creative mind to paint word pictures. He referred to the new digital business at Hearst as a chance to "work with the clay." While Hearst, in the early days of the digital revolution, didn't make large investments, in the context of my own experience building a radio broadcast company, the investments we made in start-ups seemed quite significant to me.

I had my own exposure, an often quite intimate one, with dot-com entrepreneurs. Mark Cuban, the co-founder of Broadcast. com; Steve Case, the founder of AOL; Jim Clark, the co-founder of Netscape; Jeff Bezos, Amazon's founder; and Jerry Yang, who started Yahoo, created new businesses and then acute cases of envy. I worked to a greater or lesser extent with each.

My work with Mark Cuban was especially revealing. It drew a vivid line between the old and new media.

Mark and his partner, Todd Wagner, started Broadcast.com, which, after a public stock offering, was acquired by Yahoo. The acquisition made Mark, Todd and those who invested (Hearst included) a great deal of money.

The company's business model was built around becoming a hardware and software platform for video streaming over the Internet. At the time, live video was being distributed exclusively by broadcasting, cable and satellite transmissions.

Mark was and is opinionated and forceful. He revels in provocation. We negotiated an investment by Hearst in the new company. Mark saw this as a strategic investment and was eager for Hearst Broadcasting's television stations to use Broadcast. com's platform.

Hearst Broadcasting, after the investment, negotiated with Broadcast.com but declined what Mark thought was a good deal. He was angry, let me know it in colorful terms and twenty-four hours before he was scheduled to keynote a digital conference sponsored by Hearst, canceled.

Established companies and political leaders, in the final analysis, do not like insurgents. Frequently big companies and certainly big government can organize barriers to entry that keep out the insurgents and their pesky personalities, ideas and products. The digital revolution, however, has turned out to be the irresistible force that overcame the immovable object. In the case of Mark Cuban, his anger at the broadcast establishment was simply fuel for his competitive ambitions. Today Mark owns the Dallas Mavericks and watching the early success of his friend Donald Trump has begun talking about running for political office.

As the dot-com bubble enlarged, Mark and his fellow entrepreneurs began to occupy *Forbes* rich lists and the covers of untold magazines. Amazon's Jeff Bezos even became *Time* magazine's Man of the Year for 1999. The new heroes: let's emulate them.

*Overnight rich*, with a bit of reflection, is an oxymoron, but there was no time for reflection. "Just do it" became not just an ad line for Nike, but the operative mantra.

Apropos of the times, in 1997, I began to get at least a call every other week to become CEO of some 12-to-24 month-old Internet company. The headhunters seemed to have rehearsed the offers. They all seemed to be offering around $50 million, give or take, over three years. The cash part of the offer was typically around $1 million, with the balance in stock options that would fully vest after three years. The companies, they claimed, would, well before then, be public and my 5 to 10 percent of the ownership would be worth around $50 million, which would be taxed as capital gains.

I had become a prime prospect because I was starting or investing in high-tech businesses at Hearst and the venture capitalists that had funded the start-up companies were looking for gray hair. There wasn't much of it. Many had concluded that a twentysomething, however smart, was unlikely to build lasting stockholder value. A few did, of course.

I declined. But while refusing to lead one of those conceptions, I did serve on a number of dot-com boards. While I found a lot of smart, intense and very hard-working people, I also found an eerie culture of entitlement that seemed to shadow many of the senior executives with whom I worked. They had concluded that an idea was a business and that hard work by the technology savvy would almost certainly translate into riches. They were, to say the least, impatient with more conventional views and ways.

The entrepreneurs' sense of entitlement was, at times, maniacal. They were often a youthful version of the long serving congressional committee chairman—autocratic. One CEO, whose strategy was constantly changing, careened into a rant in a late-night conversation during which I questioned his direction. Hearst was an investor and I was on his company's board. Temporary insanity would have been the plea; fortunately I was several thousand miles away on the telephone.

Another start-up entrepreneur, impatient with my less than enthusiastic response after presenting his business case for funding, checked his Blackberry for the stock price of his company and said angrily, "You obviously don't realize my stockholdings increased in value by $10 million since we started talking." I was simply asking inconvenient questions.

Impatience was endemic. Investment bankers, with their youthful CEOs in tow, would schedule meetings on top of meetings with venture capitalists and become annoyed if an immediate commitment was not made.

And often as you got to know this latest version of novelist Tom Wolfe's "masters of the universe," you realized that their overall perspective was often as narrow as a laser light.

I remember a meeting with Robert Blumberg, at the time senior vice president of Live Pics, who was trying to attract Hearst as an investor. He was showing me morphing tools, which could manipulate images. He was using the tools to change the image on Mount Rushmore and, to my annoyance, kept referring to Washington or Lincoln as "that guy" as he was maneuvering the picture of a child between them. When he removed the child, Theodore Roosevelt popped up. He asked, "Who is that guy?"

At some point, ambition's dominant tool becomes calculation. Not the numbers-work you do with a calculator, but questions like *Who wins? Who loses? Is this worth my time? Is there a personal gain in this friendship?* You have to work hard to find a counterbalance to this centripetal force.

Calculation was not absent in small-town Missouri or most business venues. But in New York, calculation is an art form. For some it is even an attraction. John Cale, the British rock musician, quipped, "I like it here in New York. I like the idea of having to keep eyes in the back of your head all the time."

And to give the mindset a bit of romance, my colleague Gil Maurer noted that gifted business leaders "can hear the music in the numbers." New York is a transactional city and the cost-benefit software is ever-present, almost regardless of the circumstances of a relationship.

My early mornings in New York periodically began with men's breakfast groups. Several were discussion groups probing for meaning beyond the day-to-day chase. I had joined similar groups in Jefferson City and Washington. In both those cities, courage and selflessness were studied, praised, and at least vaguely understood. History's heroes, saints, apostles, and even an occasional contemporary figure inspired.

• • •

While New Yorkers similarly wanted to be inspired, on many occasions the discussions turned implicitly or explicitly toward calculation. I will never forget one morning in 2002.

I was the designated discussion leader. The breakfast group numbered about a dozen and was drawn from an A-list of New York success. We met in an elegant dining room of a New York men's club and enjoyed a breakfast of eggs and bacon. I looked forward to these breakfasts. I had chosen, for that morning, a reading published by The Trinity Forum on Helmuth James von Moltke called *A Time to Stand.*

Von Moltke, a German citizen and descendant of a famous Prussian General, had been drafted into the Third Reich. He despised Hitler, but couldn't avoid military service. Von Moltke was a lawyer and ended up serving in Abwehr, the German Intelligence Service, as an advisor. At his level, he was constantly trying to reverse Hitler's course by arguing a given policy was contrary to The Hague Conventions or would invite harmful reciprocal actions.

Von Moltke believed that the only way Hitler's evil could be purged was for Germany to be defeated by the Allied Forces. He, therefore, was a friend of some who plotted Hitler's assassination, but was not a collaborator in the 1944 assassination attempt led by Claus von Stauffenberg. Shortly after the assassination attempt, those who were known to be anti-Hitler were rounded up and sent to prison to await trial. Von Moltke was sent first to Ravensbruck prison and then to Tegel, outside of Berlin. He was convicted of subversive activity and executed.

Our discussion group read from letters von Moltke had sent his wife, Freya, during the years before his death. They were deeply personal and revealed a profound faith in God.

After the readings, we turned to discussion and two friends from Wall Street argued that von Moltke had selfishly put his own life first because he was not an active collaborator in the attempted assassination. I pointed out that his series of actions had culminated in death and that at no point had he recanted to save his life. But by my ninth year in New York, I was not surprised at this characterization of von Moltke. The hard edge of New York cannot imagine selflessness. And what you cannot imagine you won't do.

The elevated levels of New York business and beyond teach you that everything is a calculation. Calculation is inexorable. Win-win results from the other guy being just as savvy as you. It gets in your blood. It bleeds into everything. In calculation's games, consideration is feigned—it is simply a tactic.

Yet at the end of the day or at least by the end of our lives, it is calculation that seems little more than a tactic. Strategy involves lines, and where we draw them reflect on us, shape the New York-Washington axis and, of course, the nation. If, in our collective lives, we eschew lines, then Washington and New York and the shifting set of alpha types will be transcendent and, guess what, overreach. We will not push back, just be forced to clean up the wreckage.

Andrew Sorkin interviewed Felix G. Rohatyn for the *New York Times* on the eve of Rohatyn's published memoir, *Dealings: A Political and Financial Life*. Sorkin refers to Rohatyn, who had a long career on Wall Street and helped save New York City from bankruptcy, as "one of Wall Street's last old wise men." Rohatyn, reflecting on his career, told Sorkin that he, like so many in the financial industry, didn't spend much time reflecting on the larger implications of his work. But he had an awakening in 1986 as he was working on the sale of RJR Nabisco:

> *The experience with RJR had caused me to rethink my traditional bankers' calculus. The bottom line was no longer simply the bottom line—the ultimate cost of the profit had to be considered. The issues Bill Anderson (a RJR Director) had raised at RJR's board meeting about laid-off employees, damaged communities, and cutbacks in employee benefits necessitated by higher corporate debt needed to be addressed.*

Rohatyn's conclusion: "The bottom line was no longer simply the bottom line—the ultimate cost of the profit had to be considered."

Yet we live in a time when the ultimate cost is too often not considered. It must be understood and remembered that employees make a material and emotional commitment to a company. The investor's commitment—capital—is important, but money is a commodity. Employees should never be treated as one. When election or re-election is the overwhelming expression of so-called political leaders and when the financial bottom line is the overwhelming expression of our financial centers, then the lines that organize our lives also destabilize and corrupt them. And they put an increasingly uninspiring face on America in a world where worldviews compete for both followers and leaders.

I am reminded of the last year Lee Atwater lived, 1991. He had engineered President George H. W. Bush's election and had infamously brought Democrat candidate Michael Dukakis down in a TV ad by associating him with the convicted killer Willie Horton. Horton had been given a furlough from prison in Massachusetts while Dukakis was governor.

Atwater, a year before his death and while chairman of the Republican National Committee, was diagnosed with brain cancer. During the ensuing year he sought spiritual counsel and ultimately apologized to his political enemies, including Dukakis.

As death neared, Atwater told a *LIFE* magazine reporter:

*Long before I was struck with cancer, I felt something stirring in American society... It was a sense among the people of the country... that something was missing from their lives, something crucial. I was trying to position the Republican Party to take advantage of it. But I wasn't exactly sure what it was. My illness helped me to see that what was missing in society is what was missing in me: a little heart, a lot of brotherhood.*

Perversely, we have reached these seminally troubling times when the only transcendent Christian voice in the public square, the Roman Catholic Church, has been badly tarnished—

although Pope Francis's direction and humility are encouraging. The other two monotheistic religions, Judaism and Islam, are at war and the latter religion seems incapable of dealing effectively with its radical jihadists. We also find, not infrequently, religion being used as a marketing scheme to create wealth for those who claim to follow Jesus, who disdained wealth.

And the inventory of *values* in our modern nomenclature is more abundant than ever. If you head a biotech firm, you get to choose from the values of Princeton's Pete Singer, who justifies post-birth abortion or the Bible, which holds life to be inviolate. If the market zeitgeist is your dominant value, you choose license, not restraint. You look for philosophers, not Apostles, and why not choose the ones untethered to a transcendent morality?

I have, you have undoubtedly observed, allowed my prose to wander into a contentious territory; a territory rife with 21st century land mines. It is this fact, not answers, that brings me to this point.

We need coherent voices of morality. We need uncompromised spiritual leadership. And returning to my world, we need for those who produce and edit and editorialize and advertise to understand that words and pictures have consequences; presumably they know this. Unrelenting direct and indirect attacks on social norms and their sources will be fatal. Unfortunately, we live in fatal times.

Morality. Objective truth. Why have we made them enemies? What would the iconic Albert Einstein say?

*Our time is distinguished by wonderful achievements in the fields of scientific understanding and the technical application of those insights. Who would not be cheered by this? But let us not forget that knowledge and skills alone cannot lead humanity to a happy and dignified life. Humanity has every reason to place the proclaimers of high moral standards and values above the discoverers of objective truth. What humanity owes to personalities like Buddha, Moses, and Jesus ranks for me higher than all the achievements of the enquiring and constructive mind. What these blessed men have given us we must guard and try to keep alive with all our strength if humanity is not to lose its dignity, the security of its existence, and its joy in living.*

If I was standing behind a podium I would, for emphasis, read those last two paragraphs again. Einstein, whose seminal work vaulted him into the top rank of scientific history, proclaimed that the lessons of great moral teachers rank higher than "all the achievements of the enquiring and constructive mind."

Today a critical mass of elites tend to reject eternal truths, regarding them as too confining while deriding religion and its assertions of morality as unthinking. This truly unthinking arrogance, asserts Einstein, is an assault on humanity.

# FATHERS

*Policies that punish men for accidental pregnancies also punish those children who must manage a lifelong relationship with an absent but legal father. The "fathers" are not "dead-beat dads" failing to live up to responsibilities they once took on—they are men who never voluntarily took on the responsibilities of fatherhood with respect to a particular child.*

**Elizabeth Brake, political philosopher**

*If we are truly to call ourselves "men" we must recognize that a defining characteristic of that word is the care and nurturing of those we bring into this world.*

**Attorney General Eric Holder**

The inevitable call came during my first year in New York. Dad, sensitized by the 1929 Great Depression and the cost of long-distance calls during much of his life, got quickly to the point. "Son," he said, "I have been diagnosed with lung cancer."

As emotions flooded my mind, Dad and I did what we always did: we quickly got to the obvious question. In this case, that question was where he was going to be treated? Sikeston's hospital was just fine for many things, but at the time lacked a single oncologist on the staff. The closest cancer treatment center was in Cape Girardeau, thirty miles away and hardly an advanced facility.

Marty and I had extra room in our apartment and quickly concluded that Mom and Dad should live with us in New York, where he could be treated at Memorial Sloan Kettering, a world-renowned cancer research and treatment center. The invitation was extended; he declined. As it turned out, he preferred a quicker death, surrounded by friends and the comfort of familiarity, to dying more slowly in some other place.

Robert Nisbet, a renowned sociologist who taught at the University of California, and who died about a year later at the same age, would have nodded approvingly and understandingly at my Dad's reaction. Dad was the antithesis of "the loose individual" that Nisbet had described as the dominant profile in a state-centered world; a person largely disconnected from place, family and other binding associations.

My Dad's reaction to my invitation can be understood on two levels. He was 82, not a good age for enduring the poisons injected into a cancer patient. But I also understood that, while he was well traveled and had an inquiring mind, he was also passionately local.

His town had cared for him and he had reciprocated. He had worked to bring jobs to Sikeston, he had worked to improve housing and medical care for the less fortunate and, importantly, he knew their faces and families and circumstances. He did not live in a social silo, he dealt up close and personal with people he would see every week of every year.

So here I was in New York, a *loose individual* in a citadel for loose individuals. Once again I was feeling the tug of my Dad's philosophy—requestioning ambition's displacement of place. Ambition and pre-occupation are kindred; it had been a long time since I had actively engaged this philosophical divide between Dad and me.

In recent years, I have thought a lot about fathers. My Dad

began our relationship insisting and later warning and finally cautioning, but always trying to lead. He began with me, then my brother, Steve, and sometimes with the larger world. His responsibilities as a father helped him form a philosophical core. It was often a useful metaphor for what was wrong with the world.

Mortality clarifies.

Until that call in the summer of 1993, Dad's principles were mostly in my mind's archives. I was, to the extent that I found time, reading Malcolm Gladwell and Jim Collins and others who framed the disruptive 21$^{st}$-century world of technology, business and management challenges. The canon of Kendall Sikes had been pushed into the background.

Shortly after my Dad's death, life according to Kendall Sikes became personal again. Marty and I began a relationship with Catherine Mercado.

Indeed, I can no longer navigate my own childhood without thinking of Catherine. Catherine occupied an entirely different world. She lived at 110th and Lexington in New York City's Spanish Harlem.

By the time my wife and I got to know Catherine, she was doing poorly in a New York City middle school. We had volunteered to become her sponsor family and make it possible for her to attend Cathedral High School, a Mid-Town Manhattan Catholic school for girls.

Catherine's early years could not have been more different than mine. Her dad was absent. Her mom was pre-occupied with the stresses of living on welfare, and had a chronic illness. TV was a constant source of noise and temptation and was in Spanish.

Catherine, as it turned out, was pre-occupied with escaping, and to her young mind, escape was a boyfriend and a job clerking at a drugstore. Her salary was converted into custom fingernails, designer jeans and costume jewelry. The pop culture beckoned; its messages were seductive.

Marty and I were neither her parents nor spectators, but as it turned out, we were more the latter than the former. While Catherine's freshman and sophomore years had been encouraging, at the start of her junior year, we saw the warning signs. Her grades began to decline and there were frequent school absences. We were, however, not unlike people looking out a third-story window at drivers speeding from opposite directions toward a common point in the same intersection, oblivious of each other.

Catherine became pregnant, dropped out of school and eventually found her way to Puerto Rico. In recent years she restarted her education in Puerto Rico and graduated from *Universidad Interamericana, Recinto deSan German*. We were overjoyed to hear the news. Marty has been able to keep up with Catherine on Facebook.

Of course, I can't prove that Catherine would have finished school in New York and delayed motherhood with a loving and assertive father. Mothers and fathers are both well aware of the hormonal tendencies of teenagers, but at least in my experience, fathers can add an important dimension to the warning. Mine did.

So, while I cannot say what would have happened in Catherine's life, I do know that even though New York has invested enormous amounts of leadership time and energy and money to break the alarming cycles of social dysfunction, progress has been modest at best. Government and private initiatives work best when the underlying culture is reinforcing. Successfully fighting a strong undertow is virtually impossible. I can recall a brief effort to resist the undertow while body surfing in Florida. The undertow won; fortunately, I was close to shore.

Realistically, private and public programs aimed at improving the chances of youth success are a modest response to an overwhelming problem.

My parents and their parents led. They set examples. They avoided hypocrisy. Dad quit smoking before he implored me not to smoke.

Mom didn't just help with homework; she, much to my annoyance, corrected my speech when it became sloppy. I can recall vividly her frustration when I pronounced *ten* as *tin*. Most importantly, she was letting me know that vocabulary and pronunciation, indeed communication, was an important skill.

Illegal drugs were available in Sikeston. At 16, I attended my first beer-bust, five years from the legal drinking age. And we know that hormonal influences on teenagers were the same in the 20th century and the 21st.

But, and this is the overwhelming change, when I grew up, society's institutions did not treat the family as a plastic social construct. Today, family in its various permutations is often a cause, not a solution.

Social activists, with their hyper-tuned antennae, find fault with any suggestion that various family configurations are not just as capable of raising well-adjusted children as a family with a caring and active father. Single parents—most often the mother—they argue, are just as capable of raising children to maturation.

Unstated, but loudly stated, is that fathers are expendable. It doesn't take two decades of study by an esteemed research institution to conclude that society is responsive. According to 2012 census data, the estimated number of fathers across the nation was 70.1 million. The number of fathers who were part of married-couple families with children younger than 18 totaled 24.4 million.

A *Newsmax* article of March 25, 2013, provided this update of marriage statistics: "Among women with less than a high school education, 83 percent give birth to their first child without being married, up from 33 percent in 1970."

Forty-seven years ago, an especially prescient report was published—*The Moynihan Report*. It was authored by Daniel Patrick Moynihan, then-assistant secretary of Labor for President Lyndon Johnson. Moynihan went on to serve as a New York senator.

Moynihan warned about the growing absence of fathers in black families and the likely social pathologies that would result. The report was quite controversial.

As James T. Patterson, a noted historian, wrote in *The New York Times*, May 28th, 2010, "Moynihan's pessimistic prophecies have come true." Patterson cited these statistics and outcomes: "Only 38 percent of black children now live with married parents, compared with three quarters of non-Hispanic white children. Many boys in fatherless families drop out of school, fail to find living-wage work, and turn to idleness or crime. Many girls become poverty-stricken single mothers themselves."

In reaction to this sad state of affairs, we get more government programs. Poverty, crime and alienation deserve response—that I understand. And some of the entrepreneurial responses in New York, such as the KIPP Academy and Harlem Children Zone are rightly acclaimed.

But maybe, just maybe, creatives should get together and ask if they can do something. Filmmakers and recording artists and others could lead the way in giving voice to Eric Holder's definition of *men*. He felt "a defining characteristic of that word is the care and nurturing of those we bring into this world." Boys or men might not have intended to become fathers when they engaged in unprotected sex, but as Holder noted, preferences aside, men have to step up and take responsibility.

Where is the creative energy? Where is the cultural leadership? Well, where is the money? Mostly, it is organized around appetites and often underwritten by advertisers with their unceasing glamorization of the commercial flotsam of life today. And cultures most important institutions—family, schools, church—have been weakened by the culture, so they are often weak countervailing forces.

And what is the likely social trajectory of the next generation of fathers? Thomas Spence, a publisher, penned a thought piece in the *Wall Street Journal* entitled: "How to Raise Boys Who Read." The article was published in September of 2010. He concluded, after reviewing books for boys which included the best seller *SweetFarts,* "One obvious problem with the *SweetFarts* philosophy of education is that it is more suited to producing a generation of barbarians and morons than to raising the sort of men who make good husbands, fathers and professionals. If you keep meeting a boy where he is, he doesn't go very far."

Today's boys will of course be tomorrow's fathers. Now I don't know whether Spence should be as exercised as he is. There is a lot of lowest-common-denominator media; whether books aimed at young people falls in that category I don't know. What I do know is that as a society we need to be careful with our children.

Mom and Dad introduced me, in my tween and teen years, to Edgar Alan Poe and Mark Twain, and on my own, I found Jack

London. It is impossible to know how these authors impacted my development, but it is likewise impossible to deny that they did. Or their literary greatness.

Today, when a gifted athlete breaks out of a potentially destructive cycle because he can hit a jump shot and then gets a few seconds on television, he mostly thanks his mother. He celebrates her ideals and tenacity. Thank God for mothers. But society needs fathers as well.

# MAXIMIZERS

*The so-called real world of men and money and power hums merrily along in a pool of fear and anger and frustration and craving and worship of self.*

**David Foster Wallace,
Kenyon College commencement, 2005**

*Some people spend their lives pursuing happiness. Poor creatures! As if they could make themselves happy by getting hold of things that are inferior to themselves. If you want peace you must get hold of what is greater than yourself, namely, of God himself.*

**George MacDonald, Scottish preacher and poet**

*The entire law is summed up in a single command: "Love your neighbor as yourself."*

**Galatians 5:14**

Some call it the Narcissistic Age. Others, seeing even more darkly, believe we are on the edge of the Nihilistic Age. Who knows? Ages are defined by historians—not commentators. However, ages happen with our complicity; we are not simply an assortment of atoms or a scientific surprise.

Cultural pessimists who use the words *narcissistic* and *nihilistic* can find evidence of both. My life's diary, which in the first few decades aligned with a more optimistic view, began to reflect on evidence that supports a more pessimistic one.

Courage in the face of strong cultural forces is infrequent and not infrequently punished. When courage is animated by "whistleblowing," corporate America is not amused. Also, it must be understood that this real world has scaled up. Abused customers most frequently end up in some form of dial around hell.

Economic and political power are increasingly concentrated in larger governments and companies, and those mammoth entities are ever more adept at protecting and extending their power. We are currently on a big-is-better binge; even young companies like Google and Facebook ramp up very quickly, fueled by global tools and ambitions along with America's remarkable capital markets.

Perhaps Walter Russell Mead is right when he concludes that "in civil society as well as in government we are in an age of empty suits and stylish haircuts on hollow heads."

But my diary is not my nature. My nature finds me looking for reasons to be optimistic. The Catholic Church has a relatively new leader, Pope Francis I. I am hopeful. I have had the opportunity to counsel with students at The Trinity Fellows Academy. I am hopeful. I have worked with young educational leaders who are alumni of Teach for America. I am hopeful. And I know that the media's hyper-infatuation with celebrities fails to capture the spirit-based generosity that is often characteristic of America.

Case in point: an associate of my wife told her about an organization in the South Bronx of New York City called Rocking the Boat. It sits along the Hunts Point shore on the Bronx River and is led by Adam Green, its founder.

The Hunts Point neighborhood of the South Bronx, according to Wikipedia, is approximately 690 acres, is a low-income residential neighborhood, has one of the highest concentrations of Hispanics in all of New York City, and "the average household income is $16,000 per year." The national average is $50,000 per year.

In neighborhoods like Hunts Point, young people are often trapped in poverty. But then there are leaders who seize opportunities.

Rocking the Boat teaches teenagers from the neighborhood schools how to build, restore, row and sail boats. Their offices and boat yard are on the Bronx River and they use the Hunts Point Park ramp as a launch.

I marvel at how counterintuitive Rocking the Boat is. I get the need to provide recreation for teenagers—but building and rowing boats? What about basketball or soccer or a skateboard park?

Yet Adam Green's leadership serves hundreds of young people annually who face serious societal challenges. They are taught to show up on time. They are taught design and construction skills while shaping boat hulls. They are taught the essential teamwork of boating. And when they face personal or family difficulties, Rocking the Boat has counselors to help them work through their difficulties.

I was recently at Rocking the Boat and, while there, picked up their packet of information about the organization. There was not a single reprint of an article from a daily newspaper. Rupert Murdoch's *New York Post*, which has the largest Bronx circulation for a daily newspaper, is too busy covering decadence to cover renewal. The latest exploits of Kim Kardashian and Kanye West take precedence.

The world's most profound commandment seeks to restrain our self-love. It implores us to think and act beyond ourselves. It came from God to us: "Love thy neighbor as thyself." Adam Green is one of millions of Americans who is doing just that.

In July of 2004, I was interviewed by a young Princeton academic, Michael Lindsay, who was doing research for *Faith in the Halls of Power*, a book published in 2008.

Michael is now president of Gordon College and updated his earlier work with *View from the Top*. Interested in what effect countercultural religious forces were playing in leader's decision-making, I turned the tables on Michael and interviewed him.

His books reflect interviews with hundreds of leaders who are also self-identified evangelical Christians. I should add since the word *evangelical* is often misunderstood, his interviewees were self-identified Christians.

"Drawing on personal interviews with an astonishing array of prominent Americans—including two former Presidents, dozens of political and government leaders, more than 100 top business executives, plus Hollywood moguls, intellectuals, athletes, and other powerful figures—Dr. Michael Lindsay shows first-hand how they are bringing their vision of moral leadership into the public square." This quick summary by Amazon leaves a very pregnant question: Who is leading and how?

In my interview with Lindsay, he estimated that only 5 to 10 percent of leaders across a broad set of disciplines made countercultural decisions. He found no countercultural decision-making in politics but the media industry offered the most. Yet I suspect all evangelical Christians today would describe themselves as countercultural.

He went on to note, "Courage is most needed on the way up as conformity pressures are greatest at that stage." Perversely, during the time employees have the least leverage, their employers are freer to shape their outlooks and attitudes.

Dr. Lindsay interviewed what I have chosen to call the 46th-floor leader. Presumably, cultural power resides on the 46th floor of an important office building. While I'm sure many of his interviews occurred well below that level, most of his interviews were with men whose status, if not actions, put them in the leadership category. There were no Adam Greens on his interview list.

I suspect, unless this universe of five hundred departed dramatically from demographic statistics, few had served in the military.

In Dad's generation, almost all young men received their first leadership training from military branches. The training was both highly structured and broadly insightful.

Dad was a part of an Army tank training battalion at Fort Knox. While I was a toddler Mom and I lived in Louisville, Kentucky, while Dad was stationed there. He then shipped out to the Asian Theater where his on-the-job education really began.

I didn't serve in the military. By the time my number came up, Marty and I had a daughter, Deborah, and I received a parental deferment.

I regret not serving.

As the years have passed, and certainly looking back, I have become increasingly convinced that real leadership that is both deep and broad cannot be produced in the several silos offered by universities and corporations. If leaders are to have a 360-degree scope, community is not optional. We need to know our neighbors. Our self-interest needs to be understood in a broader and deeper context. We need to integrate the compartments of our life.

In 1995, Robert Putman wrote *Bowling Alone*. Putman's central point was that civic engagement was in decline. His metaphor: fewer people were joining organized bowling leagues.

When I joined a law practice in Springfield in 1969, I was new to the community. Several months later, I was recruited and joined the Junior Chamber of Commerce (Jaycees). It was a young man's civic organization that had a mission of teaching young men leadership skills while working on community projects. I worked with a wide cross-section of people on civic initiatives, a youth football league, and a number of projects to help people. It was a marvelous experience in beginning leadership. It was my first leadership experience, as the law firm partners were not interested in my leading anything.

Several years ago while in St. Louis to visit family, I drove by the headquarters of Junior Chamber International (JCI), the international version of the Jaycees. When I saw the sign I did a double take, made a U-turn and walked in the front door. Since, decades before, I had been general counsel of JCI, a volunteer post, I was introduced around. And then I had my own "Bowling Alone" insight.

I asked about the health of JCI and found that in the US the number of members was about 15 percent of what it had been when I was active in the 1960s and 70s. I should have been astonished, but wasn't.

Today we tend to maximize our time on ourselves and employers—community takes time.

Community today is too often virtual. People count their

Facebook and Instagram friends while connecting to their Twitter networks. And when community is not virtual, it's often tribal—a gathering of those who share the same interests or socioeconomic status. Civic engagement that brings together people of many socioeconomic classes, views, and interests has declined precipitously.

Today's military is all volunteer. Dad, a small town guy from Southern Missouri, enjoyed talking about his Army friend from the Bronx. Dad saw the Bronx through his bunkmate's eyes and experiences before going anywhere near it. Often we speak of a person being more cosmopolitan because of their education and travels. I suspect being in the trenches during World War II taught Dad more about humanity. And the military is probably the only institution thoroughly populated across all ethnic and social lines, although relatively few leave socioeconomic privilege to join the military.

Military service is a difficult topic. Few suggest a return to conscription, and certainly today's military seems both strong and relatively cohesive. Although it is evident that back-to-back deployments in war zones exacts a terrible toll on many who serve, we still continue to shrink the number of troops available to share the load.

By contrast, American society seems more fractured and our communities more compartmentalized. Interestingly, my friends who served their nation in either the military or the Peace Corps talk often and meaningfully about their experiences.

Is there a version of divine love today, or is love in a narcissistic age too often a one-person affair? When neighbor is an abstraction, self-centered emotions are primary. We need to leave our self-sealed compartments. Among other things, we will find the world an interesting place filled with opportunities to enrich our lives.

According to historian Burt Folsom, the renowned psychologist Karl Menninger, confronted many questions on mental health. "What would you advise a person to do," one man asked, "if that person felt a nervous breakdown coming on?"

Menninger's answer: "Lock up your house, go across the railway tracks, find someone in need, and do something to help that person." Dr. Menninger's prescription reminds me of an observation by Reverend Milind Sojwal, Rector of All Angels Church in Manhattan. He noted in a recent sermon that "In God's economy there is always enough."

# REVOLUTION

*I had sat in the White House situation room, in meetings chaired by the president, where I could tell from the body language of people around the table that they had things to say and couldn't say them. They were literally buttoned up, suits and ties or military uniforms all shined up, and figuratively buttoned up.*

**James Comey, Director of the FBI**

*Mr. Obama could show some real bravery by taking on Hollywood.*

**Campbell Brown, CNN news reporter**

The setting was a Chinese restaurant in Manila. It was 1988. I was in the Philippines on federal government business, but the dinner that night was to help celebrate Butz Aquino's birthday. Butz had become a friend in 1968 at the World Congress of Junior Chamber International in Toronto.

Butz was the brother-in-law of Cory Aquino, who was then president of the Philippines; she displaced the autocratic President Ferdinand Marcos, in the aftermath of what turned out to be a relatively peaceful revolution.

While the revolution had many causes, the trigger had been the assassination of Butz's brother and Cory's husband, Ninoy Aquino, as he was returning to his country from exile to contest Marcos in 1983. Butz occupied a unique position; he was the brother of a martyr and the brother-in-law of the president.

Butz was also a powerful Philippine senator and a very popular political figure. He was in great spirits that evening and indulged his American guest with a story well known to his friends. He must have told the story numerous times, but the revelry that accompanied its retelling seemed fresh to me.

Butz had been a leader in the people-power revolution that overthrew Marcos and eventually brought his sister-in-law, Cory, to power. He had been instrumental in organizing street marches and rallies. He was not only leading a four-day revolt that culminated on February 25, 1986, he was a compelling symbolic figure. That night, he told how the popular revolution gathered force as thousands, then tens of thousands, journeyed to Manila to join the growing mass who wanted Marcos out. Each day there were demonstrations in Manila's central city, with Butz at the head of the forward phalanx.

On the day the revolution succeeded, Butz related that there were well over 100,000 people shouting for Marcos' fall. Marcos had dispatched the armed forces to break the will of the revolution and they were gathered just off the square on cobblestone streets where the troops were arrayed behind tanks. General Fidel Ramos, who would succeed Cory Aquino as the Philippine president, commanded the military forces.

Butz said that as the tank commanders were told to move forward, those at the head of the mass demonstration who were facing the tanks kneeled to a position of prayer. The tanks began to rumble forward. Butz related it was the most horrifying sound he had ever heard. One can imagine—metal tank tracks rolling across cobblestone streets. Butz said, "I wanted to run, but I looked to my left and then to my right and there were nuns kneeling and praying. I couldn't run; you know us Filipino men and face. How could I run while the nuns stayed?"

General Ramos, just as his troops reached the front line of the resistance, halted the tanks and the troops that were following them and joined the revolution. Marcos was out—Cory Aquino, the woman in the yellow dress, would replace him. And now, a generation later, her son, Benigno Aquino, is president of the Philippines.

There is no higher drama or greater cause than men and women facing down tyranny at the possible or probable cost of their lives. Americans did that over 200 years ago, then fought the Civil War over slavery and the union and, of course, since then have helped defend freedom in Europe, Asia and parts of our Southern Hemisphere. The stories of military power reluctantly exercised and of grace in the aftermath of victory need to be often told and become well known. Veterans Day needs to be more than a trip to a shopping mall.

Recent generations of Americans, however, have faced dramatically less formidable and inspiring challenges. My generation was estranged by the war in Vietnam and then concentrated on the home and self fronts. Our wars in the Middle East have been fought by volunteers, while our self-regard at home continues its upward trajectory. After September 11, 2001, all Americans were prepared to sacrifice for their country. This spirit of unity led to two declarations of war, but not one Presidential declaration of real sacrifice at home. Moral imagination was absent among the political elite.

Today, the most important clash is over the culture.

Our cultural cleavages are intense. And I am not talking about what the politicians and pundits call *culture wars* that draw combatants to the legislative or judicial arenas where they fight over social issues.

The cultural wars I am talking about swirl around what are somewhat deceptively called free markets. The first bite is free, but after that, and not infrequently, our weaknesses take over.

Bookshelves have filled in recent years on the subjects of family breakdown, obesity, illicit drugs, and various economic bubbles that have destroyed family's finances. Relatedly, we are seeing more and more written on income distribution as a cultural hinge.

But few breaking news events impact our individual or collective nervous systems as intensely as mass shootings. The Sandy Hook Elementary School massacre, featuring the indiscriminate killing of small children, is barely comprehensible. And as we struggle to comprehend and ameliorate, we too often fall back on mental illness and gun control.

Mental illness is too easy—the diagnosis is our escape. We are excused from thinking and acting in a more restorative way. Our tendency is to quickly move beyond what has become an almost existential challenge. And the stories of rampaging gunmen have become so numerous that the consequences and implications barely last over two news cycles.

I find myself in perfect alignment with the Shrewsbury, Massachusetts librarian who left me her modest estate because I took on Howard Stern while Chairman of the FCC. Words and images have consequences. Video games, for example, are not abstractions; the narrative features enemies who are to be quickly dispatched and violently so.

Sure, mass murderers' mental health is not good. We would all likely concede that to be fact. But what we have difficulty dealing with is a culture that often serves up nihilistic content to those who reject healthier cultural settings.

Nihilistic video games almost certainly entertain and preoccupy, but what else do they do? And what if anything, can society do about them?

What I learned is that the film, recording, and video game industries are very good at defending themselves. When I was pursuing shock jocks while at the FCC or characterizing Murdoch's evolving Fox Network as raunchy, the entertainment industry used parallel tracks in their counter-attacks. I was said to be trampling on the right to free speech—attempting to become a censor. The industry didn't hesitate to wrap the most egregious TV show or recording in the First Amendment. Any criticism was treated as an attack on creatives and their sacred protection. Content was conflated with the flag.

The parallel track was even more emotional and bogus. I was, it was charged, trying to force entertainment to conform to the Puritan or Victorian values of the past. I can't imagine a more quixotic undertaking.

The countervailing need is leadership that understands it is responsible for the health of the culture. Leaders who are willing to fight through the undertow. Leaders who cannot be easily bullied by status quo forces. Status quo entertainment is frequently salacious.

The status quo frequently panders to our worst impulses. It convinces us to act against our best interests in favor of their interests. The status quo, as I can tell you from personal experience, is a bully that will protect its economic wellbeing from all counterforces.

Cultural change is possible, but only with dedicated leaders pushing creative excellence and restraint. Racist laws and actions were challenged and changed. Similar boldness, at times audacity, and always deft leadership have altered traditional cultural attitudes and actions toward gays and lesbians, smokers, and, as earlier noted, drunk drivers.

I want to end on a positive note, but predicting the future is often the terrain of the foolish. I am, however, certain of two things: inertia and our self-regarding culture make it highly unlikely that countercultural change will start anywhere near the top of the pyramid. Most leaders will follow. If a strong countervailing force develops and ultimately a profound change occurs, the leadership will likely come from mothers.

As always, on the front lines of a battle, leadership decides the victor. We need a Candy Lightner, MADD's founder, in the battle against self-indulgent creatives and marketers that target children and appetites.

When Butz Aquino led the Philippine revolutionaries there was only one option—take to the streets. Thousands were prepared to die for what they thought was right. In the US, the streets are infrequently used. Occupy Wall Street was tolerated and then slowly drained of the energy necessary to effect change.

We do have, however, an intricate complex of networks and devices that facilitate organization and messages and do so in real time. And these networks are virtually impossible to shut down.

In 2050, those who write about sea changes in human conduct will report that the Internet and related networks and devices were the gunpowder of the first half of the 21$^{st}$ century. Just as the technologies associated with gunpowder often empowered political movements, the emergence of network technologies will be even more influential—indeed revolutionary. And hopefully far less destructive.

# NEW YORK SURPRISE

*Neither plenitude nor vacancy. Only a flicker*
*Over the strained time-ridden faces*
*Distracted from distraction by distraction*
*Filled with fancies and empty of meaning*

**T.S. Eliot, Burnt Norton**

*We live in a capitalist meritocracy that encourages individualism and utilitarianism, ambition and pride. But this society would fall apart if not for another economy, one in which gifts surpass expectations, in which insufficiency is acknowledged and dependence celebrated.*

**David Brooks, New York Times columnist**

We live in the *Un*-Age. Unclear. Uncertain. Unsettled. Unfinished. Everything seems to be in motion. While businesses are confronted by disruptive technologies, almost anything said to be transcendent is attacked by anthropocentric forces scattered through academia and the popular culture industries.

When I was a boy, dairies delivered milk to the home; before long, newspapers won't be delivered except by digital bits queuing in a vast electronic river.

I grew up in more settled times and sought adventure canoeing the quick streams of the Ozark Mountains. Topography, mammoth springs and jams of fallen trees combined to challenge even skilled canoeists. I can certainly recall righting my canoe on a shoal after a thorough drenching, to the laughter of my daughters, at least the ones not in the canoe with me.

Today's challenges flow like Ozark streams. And they punish those who float along the slipstreams of cultural inertia.

Spend a lot of time watching TV and you're toast. Binge on social media and you will forfeit ambition.

When I took the oath to serve as the 24th FCC Chair, there were 25 Web servers. Today the flood of Web servers continues to rise. My thesis: the power of the Internet in all of its many facets can be used and is being used as a cultural corrective.

While President Obama was using advanced targeting to reach and organize his constituency, revolutionaries in the less developed world were using the same tools to effect revolutions. Twitter and Facebook were pivotal tools in Egypt and the Ukraine. Iranian autocrats and North Korea's latest Kim attack the Internet much as their predecessors attacked radio and TV. Ultimately, they will lose.

The fact is profound change in thought leadership will likely be led by grassroots leaders. Rarely are business or government leader's conscious culture shapers—profit and reelection organize their thoughts and motivate their actions.

If more benign leadership becomes the media leadership, purchase boycotts will have been the vehicle. Financial pain will have to occur; otherwise the lowest common denominator, across much of the media spectrum, will continue to prevail—the race to the bottom will continue. On the hopeful side, at no other time have the tools to counter this force been more powerful.

The last twenty-five years of my life have been spent on the edge of the technology explosion—sometimes the knife's edge. It has been unsettling and exhilarating. But the pace of technological change can also be deceptive; we can expect too much. While these enabling and disruptive tools open up opportunities, leadership is the ultimate game changer.

Manhattan provides an unlikely but telling illustration. I discovered a very successful countercultural movement in the heart of the culture shapers' territory.

Vastly more people believe in God than deify technology, or at least that is the report from the pollsters. And through recorded history, dominant church organizations capitalized on this fact. Indeed, through much of recorded history the Catholic Church, governed from its papal center in the Vatican, was the world's dominant institution. It ruled—it made and broke leaders—and facilitated commerce. Today the Catholic Church's critical mass is in the Southern Hemisphere. How times have changed.

•••

When Marty and I moved to New York in 1993, we attended several churches close to where we lived. Our impressions of secular Manhattan were confirmed—or so we thought. The church facilities were beautifully designed and elegantly appointed, but the congregations were small and the pastors uninspiring.

We kept looking, and then one Sunday evening, at the suggestion of a friend, we attended a 6:00 pm service in the Hunter College Auditorium at 69th and Park.

The auditorium was neither beautifully designed nor elegantly appointed. The theater seating showed decades of wear. There was no altar. No cathedral ceilings. No resonant organ; just a pastor and a stage, and thankfully for my ears, a jazz ensemble.

Aside from enjoying inspired and inspiring jazz numbers, I actually found the sermon compelling and remained attentive for its extraordinary length—forty-five minutes. My tendency to become distracted went on pause. I was accustomed to 20-minute sermons with 10 minutes of content. I got over twice that in both time and content.

The church: Redeemer Presbyterian. The pastor: Tim Keller. Today, Redeemer reaches thousands each Sunday in Manhattan—*yes, Manhattan*—and additional thousands in churches both domestic and international that it helped start.

Perhaps most remarkably, Tim Keller is countercultural and, at least in New York, his congregations are filled with twenty-

and thirtysomethings that in their secular lives are cogs in the culture-making dynamic. Someday at least a few of them will be leaders, perhaps some already are.

The services take advantage of Tim's wide-ranging curiosity, scholarship, and to-the-point teaching sermons. And they take advantage of Manhattan's deep pool of talented musicians. They are not, however, reshaped along the lines of churches that seek to capitalize on a range of new computer, audio and video technologies. Substance over form. Leadership over followership.

Michael Luo, writing in the *New York Times* on February 26, 2006, noted, "Unlike many evangelicals, Dr. Keller advocates an indirect approach to change. If you seek power before service, you'll neither get power, nor serve," he said. "If you seek to serve people more than to gain power, you will not only serve people, you will gain influence. That's very much the way Jesus did it."

So, as church leaders find themselves with declining congregations and too often with embarrassing or hypocritical leadership, real leadership in religion emerges in that most unlikely venue—Manhattan.

Tim Keller became a friend, and I recall one discussion about church hierarchy and inertia. I told Tim about going to several churches after arriving in New York and finding them sparsely attended. I asked how these churches remained open. He said many, if not most, had received large bequests, which funded their operating deficits. Money so often dulls the senses; the status quo becomes the prevailing force—in and out of the church. Those who are in positions to lead simply yield to the underestimated force of money.

Tim Keller has taken on the forces that work to undermine today's church. Parents and educators should become familiar with his success.

His canon is the Bible. He does not believe that because we live in the 21$^{st}$ century we should reject the 1$^{st}$. Yet he understands the 21$^{st}$. One of Tim's indulgences is going to movies. He understands New York. He understands the inexorable pressures ignited by a 21$^{st}$-century appetite for fame and fortune. He understands the ephemeral characteristics of much that we do in our busy lives. Impactful pastoral work insists that the pastor know what is going on.

Parents and educators also need a canon shaped by more than the cultural arbiters of the day.

In my family, I can recall Mom and Dad drawing on what they called "timeless truths," and organizing life around abundance was not one of them. They enjoyed the occasional new car or washing machine or vacation, but did not define their lives by acquisition.

Our nation's defining document—the Declaration of Independence—made it clear. We were to be given the rights to pursue life, liberty and happiness. In today's world, *happiness* often translates into the pursuit of *abundance.*

An abundant life can be defined by a loving family, friends, fulfilling work, generosity or some combination of what used to be called blessings. Ironically, these characteristics often define earlier generations, or first-generation Americans, who worked so that the next generation would be better off.

Materially, I am clearly better off than my parents. My generation had the wind at its back. It didn't face the headwinds of world wars. And our nation's global competitors in Europe and Asian were mostly rebuilding their nations after the destruction of World War II. Baby Boomers could buy more—in many instances, a lot more. And for many, *better off* meant disassociating happiness from blessings; we were deserving.

Recently I was struck by a line from Federal District Judge James Spencer as he characterized the conduct of Maureen McDonnell, the wife of former Virginia Governor, Robert McDonnell. Both, while occupying the governor's mansion in Virginia, became willing participants in a pay-to-play scheme, living on much more than the governor's salary.

In sentencing Mrs. McDonnell, Judge Spencer said, "How can this woman become a person so bedazzled by material possessions that she can no longer see the difference between what is appropriate and inappropriate?"

Appropriate, inappropriate? What is or isn't appropriate is always in motion. Judge Spencer's words captured the 21st-century zeitgeist. Our parents would have said she didn't know the difference between right and wrong. Many would have defined the conduct as immoral. Those words sting. They draw vivid lines.

Indeed, in much of the world and certainly in my parents' generation, the more abundance, the more responsibility. And while my first association on the obligation of good fortune came from the Bible, there are many with no professed faiths that share their abundance through generosity. Some do so radically. There must be a transcendent spirit at work.

The Bible was translated from Hebrew to Greek, and the Greeks had a word that defined *love* as the Bible says we owe it. The word is *agape*. Agape love, roughly translated, is brotherly love.

Anger is an antonym, likewise greed and vengeance. I could go on, of course, but we all understand what separates us from the rest of the animal kingdom. We have the gift of critical thinking. We know when we have embraced blessings or received abundance without reciprocating.

It is not possible to pay even scant attention to the news without seeing or hearing the word *religion* at the top of the day's stories. We recoil at decapitation, suicide belts, and various forms of genocide, all claimed by the leaders of these benighted organizations to be religious acts. And those religious acts certainly compromise our own sense of brotherly love.

We are fighting back militarily. We have no choice. Yet if we are to play the long game, it will be necessary to use more than drones and special operation forces.

The long game is ultimately more threatening to the world's predators than farming out our countermeasures to the intelligence community and a small-armed force supplied by a technologically capable military-industrial complex.

We should always keep in mind that today's technology will ultimately be available to those who want to annihilate us. Drones are now being deployed around the world by a disparate group of nations. And non-state terrorist forces will soon find arms merchants who will sell them drones and train them in their use. It is now said that Iran has drones patterned after a US drone that went down in their territory.

And, it should always be remembered that failed or dysfunctional states will do anything to get hard currency, whether selling drugs or arms or whatever. And some of the failed states, like North Korea, have concentrated their economy on producing armaments. Arms supplies and merchants will not disappear.

The only long game that will work has to be transformational.

Today a word count would most assuredly reveal that the three most often cited religious leaders are Iran's Grand Ayatollah Ali Hosseini Khamenei, ISIS's self-proclaimed leader Abu Bakr al-Baghdadi and Pope Francis.

Pope Francis and a handful of religious leaders like Tim Keller, who walk along the same path, offer us the winning strategy. But having gone global, let me return to Manhattan.

Remarkably given the decline in church attendance among younger adults, the pews of Redeemer are filled with the young and well-educated.

Maybe I should not have been surprised; much of Manhattan is struggling with Darwinian aggression. And if you talk about spiritual concerns at work, you will be considered naïve or daft. Neither perception is helpful. Although, effective leaders can certainly use transcendent values in measuring company health.

Most Americans feel they are on a high wire every single day. Many, if not most, fear they no longer have decisive influence in their children's lives. And jobs are less secure as we export jobs and import products and turn to various automation and robotic solutions. Plus, there is a steady drumbeat from our one universal collective enterprise—the government. Translated: *Don't worry about the balance sheet, just give us more of your money so we can make government work better.*

America is full of improvisation. We call it entrepreneurship. And in the case of Tim Keller and others that follow his leadership, entrepreneurship can be countercultural. Indeed, the most consequential entrepreneur is, in one way or another, almost always countercultural.

And given the time in which we live and the challenges we face, our world, not just our commerce, could use a wholly countercultural set of entrepreneurs—leaders. We certainly need more gifted men and women in the spiritual realm. More of those like Tim Keller who are curious, scholarly, articulate, and fully disciplined by their calling. And once again, I end with Albert Einstein's words:

*Our time is distinguished by wonderful achievements in the fields of scientific understanding and the technical application of those insights. Who would not be cheered by this? But let us not forget that knowledge and skills alone cannot lead humanity to a happy and dignified life. Humanity has every reason to place the proclaimers of high moral standards and values above the discoverers of objective truth. What humanity owes to personalities like Buddha, Moses, and Jesus ranks for me higher than all the achievements of the enquiring and constructive mind.*

*What these blessed men have given us we must guard and try to keep alive with all our strength if humanity is not to lose its dignity, the security of its existence, and its joy in living.*

# THE BIG CHILL

*What is hateful to you, do not do to your neighbor. That is the whole Torah; the rest is the explanation of this—go and study it.*

**Hillel, the Hebrew elder**

Writing a book exerts an inexorable force. At its most intense—at least for me—it was the day's thesaurus. It translated what otherwise seemed ordinary events and thoughts; they all became potential pieces in a narrative puzzle. Many of those events and thoughts, of course, quickly fell to the editor's pen (mine), while others helped shape the words and phrases you have read.

An especially enjoyable and thought-provoking event occurred in the fall of 2006. Marty and I headed to St. Louis to help Jack Danforth celebrate his 70th birthday. The night after the birthday party, there was a reunion of people who had worked for Jack and with each other during the eight years he was Missouri attorney general or during the 18 years he served in the US Senate. We had gathered to enjoy food and drink and each other. It was *The Big Chill* writ large.

There were the inevitable efforts at humor, some quite good. But also interesting were the regrets. There were more than a hundred men and women in their fifth, sixth and seventh decades who had started out to change the world. This was not an assemblage of bankers or lawyers or doctors talking about their practices or how much money they made. These women and men had joined an idealistic political force to catch the bad guys or rewrite the laws and shape a more just society. And now many led businesses or law firms. Clarence Thomas was on the Supreme Court.

Jack Danforth had left the Senate in 1996, so even the most recent staff had had a chance to reflect. One of the most ambitious reflections that night was quite entertaining. A very clever song had been written and recorded by a Nashville lyricist. It was inspired and performed by a half dozen *tax LAs*, as legislative assistants were called. Jack had been on the Senate Finance Committee and these talented staffers had all worked with him on tax reform legislation.

Later on that night the musical skit had me thinking about tax policy and legislation; I guess the food had begun to dull the wine-induced euphoria. Too bad.

The Senate Finance Committee has an expansive reach. All revenue-raising legislation must move through the committee, and it touches a significant part of what the government spends. And the tax LAs worked for a senator who was well informed and motivated and worked almost seamlessly on both sides of the political aisle. Jack had strong principles and fervently held views. One of his principles was that in a legislative body, you have to work in one way or another with almost everybody. I can recall my meeting with Senate Majority Leader George Mitchell, a Democrat, during my FCC confirmation hearings. When I met with Senator Mitchell at Jack's suggestion, it was clear that Mitchell held Danforth in high esteem.

But here we were in the fall of 2006 and the committee's most direct responsibility, the tax code, was in most people's view a mess of complexity, perverse incentives and conflict. I doubt that Jack, who had spent hundreds of hours to improve the code, had a different view. Thankfully, my thoughts were fleeting and I didn't bore anybody by voicing them.

So, as we all looked back, I suspect more than a few of us heard that haunting refrain sung by Peggy Lee, "Is that all there is?" As we sought to verbally reclaim once more the glory of earlier and headier times, surely I wasn't the only one asking to what end. But reunions tend to be joyous, so my more sober thoughts would hold for another day.

Jack, in his warm and generous remarks, mused that maybe we didn't "change the world," but we had fun, gave it our best effort, and did some things along the way.

Indeed. And perhaps that is the inevitable fate of revolutionaries in a heterogeneous society rich with constitutional checks and balances. A handful of us, led by Jack, did pull off a revolution of sorts in Missouri. We opened doors and file cabinets and bank accounts; sunshine's disinfecting qualities did their work. And we used the power of litigation to check the more egregious abuses. Expectations and standards were elevated—not bad.

Washington hurdles are, however, of a different character. They are broader, higher and often impervious. Washington's grid of complexity, conflicts and narcissism is frequently impenetrable. The force of greatest strength in Washington is inertia—the status quo.

Local is, for most idealistic people at most times, the only place to start. If it should be done, start in the community, or perhaps, at the state level. Rocks skip across water and a good throw will go further than the natural laws would seem to allow. Washington is heavy water; rocks are thrown back by waves of inertia and self-interest or group interest.

Recent events in Ferguson, Missouri are instructive and dramatically so. The local government institutions in Ferguson failed. This failure between the police and black community ended up vaulting the tragic events of violence and severe racial division in Ferguson into regional, state and then national tension.

In the meantime, local polarization grew more strident, and the law enforcement and justice systems that need public support to be effective were unable to get ahead of events.

There were many articles and commentaries written about the police shooting, racial divisions, disproportionate minority representation, property damages, ransacking of local stores, and eventually a gun turned on policemen. The articles were drawn from a villain's list; there were no real heroes.

I thought one in the *Wall Street Journal* was especially revealing. Jennifer Krupp, a Ferguson resident who worked at a nearby university, told the *Journal* reporter, "Our neighborhood association meets, and who comes? The same eight people." She, on the hopeful side, said she felt recent events have "kindled more interest in taking part in local government." The result in Ferguson was a more racially balanced city council, elected by larger voter turnout.

Too often, way too often, activists operating in default mode head to Washington, not to the City Hall up the street or the State Capitol.

So here we all were, luxuriating in our memories. At a time when many recoil from earlier political associations, we were all saying how proud we were to tell others that we worked for Jack Danforth. Jack had been a countercultural leader.

Life's associations are primary. It is not possible to look back and conclude otherwise. I look back on politics because that is where I spent a significant part of my life. And it was those early associations in Missouri that made the Washington and New York chapters of my life possible.

The political life tests character every single day. Some level of self-importance is endemic. As time goes on the claque—"true believers," campaign consultants, fundraisers, big contributors, staff—engage in deification. Before long, the candidates' critics become ignorant, senseless and often enemies. And the candidate or officeholder's mix of personal traits includes at least a small element of delusion.

Journalists, in an effort to break through the carefully shaped façade, often ask candidates about their preferred reading, most influential philosophers, and the like. Campaign consultants script those answers. Indeed, in an age of gotcha politics, there is little that is not scripted.

It is clear, however, that true political leadership is not.

In January 1991, while in Los Angeles to give a speech, I visited with President Reagan at his office in Century City. Two years out of office, Reagan was relaxed and gracious. My meetings with him while he was president were very specific and in the company of other officials. I was pleased to have this opportunity to visit in a more relaxed environment.

By the time I met with him, there had been reports suggesting he was in declining health. I found him quite lucid and in seemingly good health. It was almost three years before his letter to the public announcing he was afflicted with Alzheimer's.

As I left the former president's office that winter day in 1991 I was impressed by his clarity on two quite important subjects.

I began our conversation recalling the work we had done together to eliminate an unfair doctrine constricting the free speech guarantee extended to broadcasters. The doctrine's title was Orwellian; it was called the Fairness Doctrine. I could tell by his reaction that he had bigger things on his mind, so I asked him about unfolding events in the Soviet Union as Boris Yeltsin, a Gorbachev opponent, seemed to be ascendant.

While not criticizing Yeltsin, Reagan spoke glowingly about Mikhail Gorbachev, whose leadership, character, and boldness he much admired. He spoke of their partnership and that he considered Gorbachev a truly historic figure.

One other thing left a lasting impression. When I entered his office, he greeted me and then led me to a window with a stunning view of the Pacific Ocean. He was especially pleased that this day provided an unusually clear view of the horizon, lamenting it was all too rare. Then he said of air quality, "we must do better." Those on the far right of the Republican Party, who constantly claim they are heirs to Reagan's authentic conservatism, might want to reflect on this urging to do better.

We all go through life trying to live up to something—money, power, athletic prowess, beauty, parents, and on and on. We are hounded by the illusions, fantasies, and ghosts of our imagination, which are frequently fed by culture's insistence. And as culture's noise, amplified by a nauseous proliferation of channels and devices has become deafening, confusion is hard to avoid.

In a satellite age, physical navigation is simple, navigating the prevailing Zeitgeist not so simple.

My nature is to be drawn to light. Even in the darkest moments, when death's specter predominates and only the transcendent is light, I go there. I am thankful for that force. Not only does it give me a light of hope when the dark is thick;

it provides daily ballast. And ballast is essential. The winds of life demand it—individually and collectively. But when I join the collective, I frequently feel disoriented. It takes you places that, on reflection, you wish you hadn't gone.

Purposefully, we live in a liberal society. Most of us are classic liberals; we value freedom and we give license. We too often forget, however, that personal or collective freedom can be both sublime and perverse.

Yesterday's world, while far from perfect, had a quiet yet forceful counterbalance. The family, the community, the neighborhood, churches and synagogues—they pulled us back. They forced us toward an instinctive, value-based, cost-benefit assessment in which the forces of good often prevailed. There were broken families, but fewer of them. There was addiction, but less of it. The family, while not always understanding or loving, when paired with timeless truths, checked or softened personal license as authoritatively as the Supreme Court checks the states and Congress.

Implicitly, the family, working with both public and private institutions, helped create and sustain this remarkable nation. And these institutions, even though clumsily, moved us inexorably toward a more sublime humanity.

Today the spiritual stabilizers are weakened. We forget that God made it possible for us to fail while offering us a chance for redemption. And both those who ridicule faith and those who convert its religious underpinnings to deification of self or group have weakened our individual and collective faith.

Without the possibility of transcendence, however, everything becomes disconnected, including, and perhaps most importantly, leaders. Oh, sure, there will be on occasion an above-average leader, but then we will move on. While we will build more museums and concert halls to relish the passing artistry, few will last the century, much less exert a moral force. Ultimate morality must have a transcendent origin and only its strength will assure our nation's strength and, ultimately, its perpetuity.

*Better a poor but wise youth than an old but foolish king who no longer knows how to take warning.*

Ecclesiastes: 4:13

# CLOSURE

*How small, of all that human hearts endure, that part which laws and kings can cause or cure.*

**Samuel Johnson, writer, poet**

*We may know, or think we know, and often say, that humans are "only" animals, but we teach our children specifically human virtues—evidently because we believe that they are not "only" animals.*

**Wendell Berry, author**

I watched with tears in my eyes. Loved ones all, expressing their forgiveness of Dylann Roof who had, several days before, shot one by one, to a total of nine, members of Emanuel African Methodist Episcopal (AME) Church in Charleston, South Carolina. Roof had been welcomed by the Bible study group meeting at the church and at least listened in for some period of time before he began to fire away. And now their family and friends were forgiving the shooter.

The expressions of forgiveness were taking place at a bond hearing. "It was," according to the *New York Times*, "as if the Bible study had never ended as one after another, victims' family members offered lessons in forgiveness, testaments to a faith that is not compromised by violence or grief." In our all too frequent internal contest between body and soul, the latter was ascendant.

Nadine Collier, daughter of 70-year-old Ethel Lance, her voice rising in anguish and directing her comments to Dylann Roof said, "I will never talk to her ever again. I will never be able to hold her again. But I forgive you. And have mercy on your soul."

Humanity was shocked—how could those in such emotional distress express forgiveness?

It is widely said that those who grieve seek closure—a psychological end point. Most often, or so it seems, closure is paired with arrest, trial, conviction, and ultimately punishment and the more the better. Just days before the Charleston shooting, a jury in Boston chose the death penalty for Boston Bomber, Dzhokhar Tsarnaev; friends of the victims were saying they finally had closure. While *closure* is a relatively modern term, exacting punishment is both ancient and modern.

The Charleston terrorist, Dylann Roof, had used the Confederate flag on his social media site, along with a racist screed, before his warped values led to tragedy. The shooting took place on June 17, 2015, in a state that still hung the Confederate flag in a place of honor.

As the facts were still being gathered, news commentators began to ask how long it would be before angry demonstrations and perhaps acts of violence would begin. I am sure most anticipated the kind of news coverage that had become all too common from Ferguson to New York to Baltimore. Anger was of course understandable; angry actions, many assumed, would soon follow.

And then the powerful were moved. Rather than calling out the National Guard, South Carolina's Governor Nikki Haley called her political peers and asked each to join her in calling for the removal of the Confederate flag from the Capitol grounds. In a bipartisan show of transcendent force, the state's powerful stood side by side and spoke with one voice. Days later, both houses of the state's legislature voted overwhelmingly to remove the flag.

Reflecting on this remarkable event, Scott E. Buchanan, the executive director of the Citadel Symposium on Southern Politics, noted, "The South Carolina legislature doesn't move rapidly on anything, so the fact that this has all come about is remarkable. I think we'll look back on this in future years and just be astounded," the *New York Times* reported.

The remnant of the Confederate tribe, with its myths, advocacy groups and emotional appeals was swept aside by forgiveness—by the grieving victims, African-Americans all, who had just lost their loved ones to a white shooter. And many of the politicians who had pandered to a racist subset of the South to gain electoral advantage, put down their political polls and began to be truly animated by their faith or maybe the force of faith. The Republican governor, a woman of color herself, found strength in humility.

Hard hearts had melted. Secular orthodoxy had given way to God's love. True closure.

God often seems remote and never more so than when we see bad things happen to good people. And that had just happened at the AME Church in Charleston. How can God be excused when bad things happen, especially in a religious setting?

But then God showed up in the details of one family after another. How else to explain what happened in South Carolina? Those who lose loved ones to a killer are expected to be angry, lash out—look for vengeance.

We have all been brought up short by individual acts of mercy. We have been, from time to time, momentarily humbled by the merciful. But then the world moves on and its distance from Christ's message or Moses's tablets seems more and more distant in the communities of our lives.

As this distance has increased, I have often wondered whether we have entered a world where cultural influencers believe they are the exclusive source of insight, values and power. In a self-obsessed world, can transcendence exist? As this extraordinary awakening swept Charleston and amazed the world, hope was renewed. Maybe this will help push us away from our small gods to God as a "repentant minority proved more powerful than a moral majority."

I am often frustrated by the questions that overhang

discussions about cultural change. We inflate our moment—it is, after all, the only one we have. Perhaps I risk inflating the importance of forgiveness in the aftermath of the Charleston tragedy; after all, history tells us that redemptive corrections rarely happen quickly. But then, this redemptive correction did not happen all that quickly.

In 1776 we declared, "We hold these truths to be self-evident, that all men are created equal, that they are endowed by their Creator with certain unalienable Rights that among these are Life, Liberty and the pursuit of Happiness." Yet Thomas Jefferson, who penned that profound and transcendent principle, remained anchored in the culture of his day. He remained a slaveholder. The Civil War which was fought, in part, to secure freedom for slaves ended in 1865, eighty-nine years later. The Confederate flag did not become a museum piece in South Carolina until 2015, 239 years later.

Yet we are a nation built in the aftermath of rebellion. Indeed, one of our seminal thinkers, Thomas Jefferson, called for "little rebellions." He said, "I hold it that a little rebellion now and then is a good thing, and as necessary in the political world as storms in the physical."

We are a nation that provides space for the rebellious. In both commercial and social affairs we tend to call little rebellions entrepreneurship. Yet in political affairs, we have reached a state of entropy, as rigid two-party rules combine with special interests and both resist any change that will eliminate or compromise their interest.

What we need are activists that blend the profound social and political foundations of the past with the adventures of the future. And we need the faithful to embrace forgiveness, to be light in darkness. We need heroes. Recall the words of Katherine Lee Bates, who in 1904 wrote *America the Beautiful:*

> *O beautiful for heroes proved*
> *In liberating strife,*
> *Who more than self their country loved,*
> *And mercy more than life!*
> *America! America!*

*May God thy gold refine*
*Till all success be nobleness,*
*And ev'ry gain divine!*

# QUESTIONS FOR DISCUSSION

THE POET, DANA GIOIA, suggests we are all following a downhill path and are often surprised by where we are and how we arrived. Dana's poem on page 25 is a good starting point in beginning a conversation. And if you would like to go beyond your discussion group, please join me on alsikes.com. I'm also available to speak to book groups via telephone or Skype (contact me via the website.)

1. Each of us encounters dozens, if not hundreds, of stories each day through advertising, news and entertainment. How influential are these stories in our lives—for the better or worse? Do we have any ability to influence the messages?

_____

_____

_____

_____

_____

2. My Mom and Dad began their parenting by insisting and then suggesting and finally cautioning. Is the family losing its preeminent role of influence in children's lives? Is there any way government can create effective institutions that can serve as surrogate parents?

_____

_____

_____

_____

_____

3. Does society need spiritual stabilizers? If stabilizers become stronger, how will that likely have occurred?

_____

_____

_____

_____

_____

4. Mass shootings have become regular events. Are these shootings primarily a result of individual mental illness? Does our culture play a role? If so, what are the cultural forces and is it possible to reverse their influence?

_____

_____

_____

_____

5. Polls unequivocally reflect distrust or worse in the institutions of government. In today's money and poll centric political culture, is it possible to affect and sustain favorable government?

_____

_____

_____

_____

_____

6. If more trusted leadership emerges, what will be the contributing circumstances?

_____

_____

_____

_____

_____

7. Sixty-five years ago America elected a President who had never held elected office–Dwight Eisenhower. Many seem ready to elect another one–Donald Trump. What developments do you believe helped lead to Trump's popularity?

_____

_____

_____

_____

_____

8. What is the relationship between the size of government and the potential of a trusting citizenry?

_____

_____

_____

_____

_____

9. Do leaders shape the culture or are they more likely to be shaped by it? What examples of leaders re-shaping cultural forces come to mind?

_____

_____

_____

_____

_____

# ACKNOWLEDGMENTS

Drawing on parents and friends, opportunities and experiences, and a range of thinkers and writers in an effort to make sense of life is far more complicated than I thought.

I had the good fortune of working for or with some consummate leaders including Jack Danforth, Kit Bond, Mac Baldrige, Ed Meese, Al McDonald, Frank Bennack, Gil Maurer, Peter Flanigan and, of course, the two presidents I served, Ronald Reagan and George H. W. Bush.

I feel especially blessed to have friends who read one or more of my earlier drafts (and there were many) and gently criticized while giving me abundant encouragement. In first position is my wife, Marty and then my daughters, Debbie, Christy and Marcia. Thanks also to Os Guinness, Bill Edgar, Joe Loconte, John Mathis, Ron Sauder, Mike Phillip, Chelsea Horvath, Caleb and Shannon Armbrust, Tracy Mehan, Judith Reveal, Steve Sikes, Lorrie Secrest, Bunky Wright, Syman Stevens, Alex Netchvolodoff, Ken Robinson, Mark Berner, Anne Adler, Gina Otto, Tom Woodbury, Doug McCormick, Richard Marks and Carol Miller.

I also had fun with the cover art—at times to the frustration of John Koehler, the name sake Publisher of Koehler Books. Shannon McNary, Amy Haines, Richard Marks, Barbara Jaffe, Karen and John Mathis, Bob and Dellie Brell, and Anne and Doug Adler served as my focus group. They had, thanks to John Koehler and his artists, some very good options.

And finally thanks to Joe Coccaro, my editor, who insisted and then counseled and finally agreed, plus Shari Stauch who opened the world of social media to help spread the word and sell books.

CPSIA information can be obtained at www.ICGtesting.com
Printed in the USA
BVOW03*1444310316

442364BV00001B/2/P